Collaboration

PHILOSOPHY OF EDUCATION IN PRACTICE

Series Editors: Marit Honerød Hoveid, Ian Munday, and Amy B. Shuffelton

This series of short form books explores issues, topics, and themes that are foundational to educational practices both within and beyond the boundaries of formal education. With books on topics such as collaboration, responsibility, touch and emotions, the series generates philosophical discussions of education that are accessible to the curious reader and draws out commonalities and differences in thinking about and doing education across cultures. By addressing educational thought and practice in a philosophical manner the series encourages us to look beyond prespecified "learning outcomes" and asks us to slow down and explore the messiness and complexity of educational situations.

Advisory Board:

Also available in the series:

Forthcoming in the series:

Collaboration

Philosophy of Education in Practice

AMY B. SHUFFELTON

BLOOMSBURY ACADEMIC
LONDON • NEW YORK • OXFORD • NEW DELHI • SYDNEY

BLOOMSBURY ACADEMIC
Bloomsbury Publishing Plc
50 Bedford Square, London, WC1B 3DP, UK
1385 Broadway, New York, NY 10018, USA
29 Earlsfort Terrace, Dublin 2, Ireland

BLOOMSBURY, BLOOMSBURY ACADEMIC and the Diana logo are
trademarks of Bloomsbury Publishing Plc

First published in Great Britain 2024

Series design by Grace Ridge
Cover image © Tyas drawing / Getty Images

A catalogue record for this book is available from the British Library.

A catalog record for this book is available from the Library of Congress.

ISBN: HB: 978-1-3503-0274-7
        PB: 978-1-3503-0273-0
        ePDF: 978-1-3503-0275-4
        eBook: 978-1-3503-0276-1

Series: Philosophy of Education in Practice

Typeset by Integra Software Services Pvt. Ltd.
Printed and bound in Great Britain

To find out more about our authors and books visit www.bloomsbury.com
and sign up for our newsletters.

CONTENTS

Series Editors' Foreword vi
Acknowledgments ix

1 Collaboration: An Introduction 1
2 Friendship and Loyalty 21
3 Responsibility and Power 43
4 Collegiality and Consent 69

Notes 84
References 93
Index 96

SERIES EDITORS' FOREWORD

It is a common enough experience for both educators and those being educated to find themselves bamboozled, bothered or discombobulated by the kinds of thing that happen during educational encounters and settings. Trying to understand such experiences and acknowledge their meaning and import is something that can nag away at us. We hope that readers who are drawn toward exploring such concerns will find this book and the series to which it belongs helpful in developing a deeper and more nuanced understanding of educational practice. Addressing educational thought and practice in a philosophical manner takes us beyond the sanctuary of prespecified "learning outcomes" and asks us to slow down and explore the messiness and complexity of educational situations.

This series aims to explore the connections between thinking and doing in education through a variety of philosophical lenses. Authors will address diverse issues, topics, and themes in multiple contexts from a variety of perspectives. Throughout this series we hope to elucidate the commonalities and differences in thinking and doing education across and between cultures. What holds the series together is not a particular point of view but instead a shared emphasis and approach. Each book will connect experiences (doing) and enduring questions in philosophy of education (thinking) to explore a major concept in education. Recent philosophical work has not shirked a concern with educational virtues and values, but its treatment of these matters is sometimes narrowly academic. We believe that educators, administrators, policy professionals, parents, and other citizens curious about education would benefit from a broadly accessible, yet rich treatment that offers fresh perspectives on enduring dimensions of education. While the series is designed to speak to practitioners, who are interested in reading theoretical work, the books in this series are not intended as "how to" guides—we would not presume to lecture to those working in the field, or attempt to find hard and fast solutions to educational problems. Rather the authors in the series aim to philosophically inhabit practice and offer meditations on alternative ways of thinking/doing which arise from their research or teaching within the current neoliberal, globalized context.

Series editors,
Marit Honerød Hoveid
Ian Munday
Amy B. Shuffelton

Volume one: COLLABORATION

In the first volume of the series Amy B. Shuffelton explores the theoretical and practical dimensions of "collaboration." "Collaboration" has been a buzzword in the educational literature for some time and is generally presented as something wholly positive, a term to be treated with nothing but frothy approval. As Shuffelton shows, things are not so straightforward. "Collaboration," in contrast to cooperation, has a dark aspect—gangs of thieves collaborate and in the Second World War, residents in various countries "collaborated" with the Nazis. It can involve selling out and submissiveness in the face of unequal power relations. Drawing upon film, literature, and real-life practical examples, Shuffelton shows how this darker hue to collaboration, often surreptitiously, colors the culture of schooling. She explores this in relation to classroom relationships and the wider neoliberal culture of schooling. In revolt against the darker aspects of collaboration she offers a compelling vision of collaboration, which is optimistic, yet resistant to the idealistic framing of the concept typical in much research. The word "labor" is literally built into the word collaboration and good examples of collaboration in practice necessarily involve a degree of struggle. Learning to work well with other people, friends or otherwise is rarely a smooth or straightforward endeavor.

Collaboration has a strong international flavor. The discussion draws upon philosophical work from a variety of traditions. The book features Hungarian cinema and British Children's literature, including the trials and tribulations of Harry Potter and friends. The most central "comparative" aspect to the book involves scenes and stories taken from the author's experience of working with children on collaborative projects in Poland and the United States. Shuffelton details how the rolling out of an interdisciplinary project, the Village program conducted with students from both contexts, embodied the rich possibilities for agency and taking responsibility, which good forms of collaboration may engender.

ACKNOWLEDGMENTS

I've been thinking about "good collaborators" since I entered the University of Wisconsin Madison's Educational Policy Studies program in 1997 and I started hearing that combination of words, which after a year and a half in Polish public school struck me as odd. Having taken several decades to figure out, this book exists thanks to more collaborators than I can name here, whose friendship, conversation, and support contributed to its creation. Thanks first to the teachers and students of Szkola Podstawowa 116, especially Olaf Solarz and family, who introduced me to friendship and solidarity as those played out in a Polish school. Enormous thanks to my graduate advisor and friend ever since, Daniel Pekarsky, who pressed me to think harder about all of the above. As Editor-in-Chief of *Educational Theory*, Chris Higgins invited me to submit my article on collaboration to a symposium, which laid the groundwork for this book. Conversations with Chris have enriched this project and a lot else. Thanks to all my philosophical collaborators, especially Samantha Deane, Derek Gottlieb, Heather Greenhalgh-Spencer, Kathy Hytten, Kathleen Knight-Abowitz, Cris Mayo, A.G. Rud, Kurt Stemhagen, Barbara Stengel, and Sarah Stitzlein. True friends appear more than once every few hundred years; Jessy Randall and Atissa Banuazizi are my evidence. I couldn't have written this book without you both. Heartfelt thanks to my family, Noah Sobe and Philomena and Maisie Shuffelton-Sobe, who built villages with me (Noah), shared enthusiasm for small places and how they work (Philomena), and chopped all the vegetables with the verve that makes her exceptional (Maisie). My mother, Jane Shuffelton, career teacher extraordinaire, has always reminded me what really matters in schools and why schools matter. (Hint: it's not the regulation of chewing gum.) This book is dedicated to her.

CHAPTER ONE

Collaboration: An Introduction

Harmony and Conflict

To the sound of a children's chorus, Zsófia silently creeps down the school corridor. On her face, rapt attention to the music competes with the wariness of a child encountering her new school for the first time. "Our voices spread their wings to grant your wish for a thousand beautiful things," the children sing in harmony. "All sorrow, all worries, all the sadness shall vanish within the beautiful rays of love." Zsófia peeks through a door left slightly ajar into the rehearsal room, then ducks back half-hidden to listen, until, hearing adult footsteps, she runs back to join her mother and the school principal on their tour of the school. In this opening scene of the short Hungarian film *Mindenki*, the chorus's assurance of a utopia in which "our voices" pave the way to desire's fulfillment and sorrow's disappearance is echoed by the principal's proud commitments. The camera catches him finishing up a comment to her mother, "to make it easier for her to fit in," and then he turns to Zsófia to ask if she saw anything interesting. When she nods shyly, he proudly tells his two guests that the school's chorus wins prizes every year and that Zsófia will be able to join it if she wishes. He insists, he says, that the chorus be open to all who wish to join.[1]

The first minutes of Zsófia's first day at school suggests a more ordinary, less utopian, social reality. A boy serving as the classroom monitor adds her name to the list of misbehaving students on the board before the teacher enters the room, though Zsófia is quietly seated at her desk. With the brisk efficiency of a practiced educator, the teacher pays no attention, wipes the names away, and introduces Zsófia before launching into a lesson on the regions of Hungary. Thwarted, the boy turns to hassle Liza, who whacks him on the head with a notebook when the teacher's back is turned. Zsófia turns and meets Liza's eye, they share a grin, and a friendship begins. This, as shown by further scenes of children playing clapping games on the playground, squabbling over who gets to sit next to whom at lunch, and sharing special treasures, is a typical primary school. The familiar concerns of childhood mix with its glories as Liza and Zsófia forge their friendship through a shared love of music.

The prize-winning chorus, however, makes this school story extraordinary. It turns out that the chorus director manages to win prizes while including everyone by allowing only some children to sing. The rest, including Zsófia, are told to mouth the words silently. Zsófia is crushed. Told by the beautiful and glamorous director, Ms. Erika, that no one needs to know about this, she is too embarrassed to tell even Liza, until Liza notices her friend's low spirits and figures out what is going on. Liza confronts Ms. Erika, who tries to shame both Liza and all the silenced singers into continued compliance, but Liza will no more accept her chorus director's abuse of authority than she accepted the classroom monitor's petty tyranny. After that day's rehearsal, all the children leave the building in pensive silence, and Zsófia throws an arm across her friend's shoulder. "This is so unfair," says Liza to her friend, back at Zsófia's house. "We should all be allowed to sing." A flash of emotion crosses Zsófia's face, and she responds "I think I have an idea."

The rhythmic percussion of children's clapping games is the soundtrack to the next frames, which portray Liza and Zsófia making their way through the school's informal spaces: talking to girls playing on the playground, talking to boys kicking a ball, talking to a couple of children in a shadowy staircase, passing notes. Then, in black and white concert dress, the children head to the performance in disciplined silence. The singer before them finishes her performance, and Ms. Erika calls the chorus onto the stage. Liza's and Zsófia's hands join in a squeeze, and Ms. Erika lifts her baton. In perfect silence, the entire chorus mouths their song. Flustered, Ms. Erika puts her baton down, furiously whispers "What's going on? Sing!" at them, and tries again. Only after Ms. Erika storms off the stage in humiliated defeat does the chorus sing aloud, opening with Liza's solo voice and then, as smiles slowly cover the children's faces, all singing together.

By the time *Mindenki* was released in 2016, the Hungary of the early 1990s in which it is set had been replaced by a new vision of social and political life. In the first years after the collapse of Soviet-backed communist regimes, Hungary, like other former satellite states in Eastern and Central Europe, celebrated its newfound freedom from oppressive, authoritarian control. Citizens could lift their voices. The combined forces of liberal democracy, European unification, and a market economy would send thousands of beautiful things their way. As it happened, this vision of collective harmony proved fleeting. By 2010, with the election of nationalist leaders who quickly curtailed press freedoms and judiciary independence, Hungary's liberal democratic vision was replaced with a very different vision of what holds people together. Nativism seeped into the cracks globalization made in the national self-image; "soft autocracy" replaced liberal democracy. Intelligent observers were reminded that history does not march inexorably forward toward any particular vision of progress, and that societies need constantly to reinvent the terms under which they hold together. While *Mindenki* can be enjoyed simply as a film depicting the joys and struggles of children's lives in schools, it is also a paean to ideals of collectivity that uphold human equality, freedom of expression, and democratic governance.

Primary school makes a terrific setting in which to stage stories of conflict between incompatible visions of collective harmony. Schools, after all, are the places where children learn how to work and live with people who are not necessarily kin or personal friends. Schools, that is, are where future citizens learn to collaborate in the public sphere. Furthermore, schools are where children learn what kinds of collaboration their community praises and what kinds are frowned upon. They learn which are the times and places for working together, and which for keeping one's eyes fixed on one's own work. In addition to *how* and *when* to collaborate, children learn *with whom*, and how people are grouped together for particular kinds of activities, officially and unofficially. They learn who exercises authority and what one stands to gain or lose by one's decisions to thwart or follow it in various circumstances. These are the questions this book addresses, as ethical rather than merely practical matters. With whom do we have a responsibility to collaborate, and how? What configurations of authority promote the kinds of collaboration that enable us to live together well? In addressing those questions, the following chapters also emphasize their unavoidability. Not only does failing to consider how we work together open the door to collaborations that are trivial or even harmful, it also matters *that* we work together.

Collaboration's Ethics

Because this book treats collaboration, by which I mean the ways we work together in sustained relationship, as an ethical rather than merely practical matter, a brief detour is in order. Before taking a deeper dive into collaboration itself, the reader deserves to know on what grounds the text is using normative language—words like *responsibility*, living together *well*, and collaborations that can be *good, trivial, or harmful*. What gives collaboration ethical valence? The chapters that follow draw on a number of thinkers, and throughout the book I have aimed more to suggest a variety of perspectives than to provide systematic answers, but the ideas presented are patched into something of a crazy quilt framed on John Dewey's ideas about democracy. For Dewey, democracy meant more than a system of government. Rather, it represented what he called a "mode of associated living," a mode worth striving for because it enabled human beings continuously to grow. This growth was, for Dewey, of a piece with education. What Dewey means by education is by no means limited to what happens in schools, but schools are exceptionally important sites for both passing along and improving upon whatever a society has figured out about how to live together. "All that society has accomplished for itself," in Dewey's words, "is put, through the agency of the school, at the disposal of its future members." And school is the meeting point of a society's past and future. "All [society's] better thoughts of itself it hopes to realize through the new possibilities thus opened to its future self."[2]

Society, Dewey recognizes, "is one word but many things."[3] The word can be used descriptively, to denote any assemblage of persons, or normatively, to connote positive qualities of association such as "praiseworthy community of purpose and welfare, loyalty to public ends, mutuality of sympathy."[4] Across decades of writing about schools and societies, Dewey's definition of the kind of society he calls democracy adds shades of nuance, but his core insight stays remarkably consistent. In *The School and Society* (1890), he defines society as "a number of people held together because they are working along common lines, in a common spirit, and with reference to common aims. The common needs and aims demand a growing interchange of thought and growing unity of sympathetic feeling." In *Democracy and Education* (1916), Dewey's titular terms each replace the descriptive (school, society) with the normative (education, democracy), or, to use Dewey's word, the eulogistic. At their best, societies are democracies; at best, what schools provide is education. In the quarter century since Dewey had arrived at the University of Chicago, started his famous Laboratory School and begun writing extensively about education, he had been attending to uglier aspects of society. Corrupt political machines had tightened their control over rapidly diversifying Northern cities. Robber barons had accumulated extraordinary sums while indigenous people were displaced, urban slums grew, and workers' attempts to unionize were violently repressed. Women were consistently denied suffrage, and Jim Crow repression strangled democracy in the South. World War had brought a wave of jingoistic nationalism to the United States. It was impossible to ignore

> the facts which the term [society] denotes ... not unity, but a plurality of societies, good and bad. Men banded together in a criminal conspiracy, business aggregations that prey upon the public while serving it, political machines held together by the interest of plunder, are included. If it is said that such organizations are not societies because they do not meet the ideal requirements of the notion of society, the answer, in part, is that the conception of society is then made so 'ideal' as to be of no use, having no reference to facts.[5]

If gangs, corporations, clans, social sets, political parties, and other exclusionary groups are each a mode of "working along common lines," that is collaborating, that involves sympathetic communication and loyalty to common aims—and Dewey recognizes that, loath though their critics may be to admit it, they are—how can we say any form of society is more commendable or objectionable than any other? One approach to gauging societies' merits, which John Rawls later came to call "ideal theory," is to conjecture, present the rational grounds for, and subject to public scrutiny an ideal mode of affiliation.[6] As the polestar guided maritime navigation, that ideal could then guide human actions in the real world. Without imagining that we could reach the theorized ideal itself, any more than a sailor believes following the stars will get him *to* the stars, such an ideal would offer the certainty of guidance to good harbors. Among the philosophical analyses that treat education and society as mutually constitutive, Plato's account in the *Republic* and Jean Jacques Rousseau's in *The Social Contract* and *Émile* exemplify this ideal approach. Dewey suggests a different means of finding a measure that will guide our actions. "We cannot set up, out of our heads, something we regard as an ideal society," he says. "We must base our conception upon societies which actually exist, in order to have any assurance that our ideal is a practicable one .... The problem is to extract the desirable traits of forms of community life which actually exist, and employ them to criticize undesirable features and suggest improvement."[7]

If any social group, says Dewey, is to count as more than a mere assemblage (like a school of fish, or a constellation of stars), it will share, and share a consciousness of, some interest held in common. In addition, because no genuinely social group includes everyone, each social group needs to interact with other groups. "From these two traits," says Dewey, "we derive our standard. How numerous and varied are the interests which are consciously shared? How full and free is the interplay with other forms of association?"[8] The reason—the only reason—to prefer democratic social arrangements, according to Dewey, lies here: "these two traits are precisely what characterize the democratically constituted society."[9] In both *Democracy and Education* and in his later recap of his educational ideas *Experience and Education* (1938), Dewey uses a gang of thieves as the counter example to democracy. A gang of thieves is a society, undeniably. It contains shared interests, and possibly even full and free interplay of ideas within the gang. When it comes to interactions with other forms of association, however, the need for deception limits thieves' options. Societies founded on despotism and privilege also fall short because they limit interaction. Stark divisions between sub-groups within a larger society limit the free play of ideas, to the detriment of all. "The more activity is restricted to a few definite lines—as it is when there are rigid class lines preventing adequate interplay of experiences—the more action tends to become routine on the part of the class at a disadvantage, and capricious, aimless, and explosive on the part of the class having the materially fortunate position."[10] That expansion of the example of thieves to all instances of "rigid class lines" invites the reader to consider the harm caused by any rigid divisions, including those that plague contemporary democracies—divisions by race, for instance, by religion, and by immigration status.

The Public and Its Problems (1927) reiterates this insight once more, this time in the context of an analysis of democracy that distinguishes *state* apparatuses, for example laws, offices, procedures, from the *democracy* such apparatuses are meant to enact and preserve. "Wherever there is conjoint activity whose common aims are appreciated as good by all singular persons who take part in it, and where the realization of the good is such as to effect an energetic desire and effort to sustain it in being just because it is a good shared by all, there is in so far a community," says Dewey. "The clear consciousness of a communal life, in all its implications, constitutes the idea of democracy."[11] In this interpretation, democracy is not a permanent state of affairs. It "is not a fact and never will be."[12] Neither is there, nor has there ever been, "community" as a perfected and stable state of affairs. What Dewey's definitions allow us to do, however—or so he claims, and I find useful—is to consider moments of associated living that approximate, that tend toward, this conception of democracy. The children's chorus in *Mindenki*, for instance, experiences such a moment when the children realize that they face a shared problem and together work out a way to solve it. They come to an agreement that the practical exclusion of some members' voices is unacceptable to them, they refuse to accept Ms. Erika's authority, and they find a way to sing together. The film ends with their moment of perfect unification of voice and purpose, and its viewers are spared the inevitable diffraction to follow. By Monday, the viewer knows to expect, the class monitor will go back to pranking his peers and Liza will find ways to put him in his place. Instances of democracy never last. But the education they provide perhaps does.

How We Collaborate

Dewey regularly refers to democracy as a kind of work or activity. In *The School and Society,* society means "*working* along common lines"; in *Democracy and Education* democracy is "conjoint, communicated *experience*"; in *The Public and Its Problems*, the realization of shared interests effects "an energetic desire and *effort* to sustain it."[13] The word "collaboration," whose Latin roots are *co-* (together) and *laborare* (to work), is one way to capture this idea of associated living as a kind of ongoing work, an effort. It might also be called cooperation, but the word collaboration has connotations that make its frequent use in schools and other workplaces especially interesting. In contrast to cooperation, collaboration hints that the work is difficult, *laborious*. In *The Human Condition*, a mid-twentieth-century take on what holds societies together, Hannah Arendt distinguishes between two kinds of work, and she notes the curious fact that most European languages contain two words for work that reflect this distinction. The kind she calls labor responds to the incessant demands of everyday life. Cooking is labor; bathing babies is labor; mining coal is labor. Labor's accomplishments are used up almost as soon as they are completed, and a new effort needs to be undertaken as soon as the first is finished. The food gets eaten; the baby gets dirty; the coal gets burned. In contrast, work produces *works*, of art or architecture or craft. For Arendt, politics falls into neither of these categories. Instead, she calls it *action*. In calling it that, she, like Dewey, perceives it to be ongoing, though her vocabulary takes the sense of laboriousness out of it. Without belaboring here the question of whether Dewey is right to treat politics as a kind of work or Arendt to hold work and politics separate—though it's an interesting question for sure—we can take up Arendt's reminder that attention to words and their uses serves as a point of entry to thinking about how we do things together and how we think about what we're doing. Arguably, the Latin roots of cooperation, *co* (together) and *operare* (to work, in that second sense Arendt points out, the creation of a lasting thing, an *opus*) are already a hint to why collaboration is used more often to describe teamwork. Living together with others requires constant labor, producing nothing lasting, no opus, except the chance to keep on living together.

Accordingly, this book considers the uses and connotations of the word "collaboration," which has become something of a buzzword of late, as a point of entry to thinking about how schools teach children to do things together. Like Dewey's "society," "collaboration" can be used to describe students' joint endeavors in both descriptive and normative visions of community. In *Mindenki*, schoolchildren enact a subversive democratic self-governance as they *collaborate* to come up with an effective response to Ms. Erika's bullying. They work together to create and carry out a plan that honors their self-respect, their mutual esteem, and their love of music. As the children are persuaded by Liza and Zsófia to take action, they communicate via their relational networks, talking and passing notes. They organize in the spaces that are difficult for teachers to surveil and control, such as playgrounds, staircases, and hallways. When the chorus pulls off its plan, the viewer is presented with an idealized normative portrait of what people can accomplish if they work together to solve a shared problem. As the children sang at the start of the film, all sadness and all sorrows vanish. This is a moving picture of collaboration at its best.

Yet the chorus members' initial compliance with Ms. Erika's demands that they silence themselves can *also* accurately be described as *collaboration*. Until they decide no longer to do so, the children work with Ms. Erika to maintain the deception that the chorus is open to all *and* able to win competitions year after year, a remarkable achievement that none of the adults seems to question. In upholding this pretense, they keep one another silent. Their collaboration gives Ms. Erika's authority its grip. Until they finally refuse to do so, Zsófia and the other silenced students presumably comply in order to gain a sense of belonging and the prestige of being part of a winning team, as well as to avoid the humiliation that Ms. Erika shows herself willing to unleash if anyone challenges her. As Liza's decision to speak up shows, their collaboration with Ms. Erika was undertaken on the students' own volition and was also challengeable at any moment. In one sense, nothing prevented any of the children from speaking up at any point, though Ms. Erika's ability to deflect the blow and turn it back onto Liza demonstrates the hazards of dissent. And of course none of the adult members of the school community seemed to question the extraordinary circumstances of the chorus's improbably fortuitous harmonization of equality and excellence. They were, if not collaborators exactly, certainly complicit. Collaboration, while at its best a means of accomplishing goals that are both shared and good, can also entail working together in ethically troubling ways toward problematic ends.

The more sinister configurations of how people work together, typically in situations of unequal power and under the thumb of oppressive authorities, are familiar to speakers of many European languages—including Hungarian—via the many cognates of the word "collaborator." Since the Second World War, "collaborator" has been used in a pejorative sense, referring to persons who work with an authority widely perceived as hostile to the interests of the group, usually to earn special privileges for themselves and perhaps for their families. In French, *collabos* cooperated with the Nazis during their occupation of France. In Polish, a *kolaborant* could be someone who cooperated with the Nazis or with the Soviet Union-backed communist regime. Curiously, the word rarely has this nuance in English, in which children and teachers are casually encouraged to be "good collaborators." The atypically positive connotations of the word "collaborator" in English might be an effect of political history. Anglophone nations— Australia, New Zealand, the UK, Canada, and the United States—have never in modern history been invaded by foreign powers, and thus have never had to contend with an occupying authority. More accurately, that is the story from the perspective of the English and their descendants who established these nations. The Maori, Irish, Ojibwe, Puerto Ricans, and others who were invaded by English-speakers might be less inclined to see matters in the same way, as might English-speakers in Nigeria, Jamaica, India, and other colonized nations. Yet, with the English-speaking majority coming out on top and, importantly, organizing school systems that teach historical narratives in which Anglophone citizens excluded no one yet still won all the geopolitical prizes, teachers, children, and parents can be encouraged *to collaborate* as if that word raised no questions.

After teaching in a primary school in Poland for a few years in the 1990s, I was astonished to hear professional educators back in the United States talk about teaching students to be "good collaborators." In Polish schools, that appellation would have been as nonsensical as telling someone to be a "good snitch." Rather, Polish teachers told children to be good *koledzy*, a cognate of "colleagues" that carries the sense of friends, not one's closest friends but the wider group that English-speakers would also call, loosely, friends, or maybe acquaintances, for example, classmates, business associates, neighbors. When students tattled on classmates for cheating, I heard their teachers tell them that it was no way to treat your *koledzy*. This rebuke functioned to make an ethical point about loyalty to peers and cooperation with authorities. It told children that *disloyalty* was the serious ethical breach in such instances, where American children would likely have been thanked for their honesty and then advised to mind their own business.

An awareness of the dark side of collaboration is lost in the blithe Anglo-American enthusiasm for collaboration in schools. Why does this matter? Because with it is lost a set of important educational ideals having to do with judgment and responsibility, involving the balance of potentially conflicting loyalties. Reckoning with those complicated problems of judgment, responsibility, and divided loyalties, this book aims to show, is a key aspect of preparing children to live in societies that not only share numerous and varied interests *but also* remain open to interactions with other groups. My point is not that the word "collaboration" itself is somehow a problem. Rather, the word's mixed implications, combined with the curious fact than in English its connotation of selling out in the face of inequitable power arrangements is mostly ignored, raises important questions about what schools are asking for—and what they are ignoring—when they celebrate "collaboration."[14]

The human inclination to collaborate, this book maintains, inspires our best actions as well as our worst. Collaboration makes us friends and allies, colleagues and citizens; it enables us to keep on living together. It also drives exclusionary politics and, at its very darkest, leads us to throw those we consider "other" under the bus for the sake of those we consider our own. These are flip sides of the same coin of human sociability, of our need to live in relationship with others. "Our own" can be, at its most morally despicable, just me, although it takes extraordinary circumstances—some mix of terror and pathology—to make people sell out their nearest and dearest. Human beings prove quicker to deny their affiliations and protections to those farther from them, and for all the aspirational cosmopolitan language of religion, philosophy, and the United Nations, almost no one considers all of humanity "my own" in any deep way. I might protest that I do, but when push comes to shove, the needs of my closer own—my family, my neighborhood, my nation—typically come first. And in some sense they must because if I really treated my friends as deserving no more of my care than strangers on the opposite side of the globe, I couldn't really call them my friends at all. In the best political arrangements, of course, Dewey's full and free interplay with other forms of association encourages me to recognize my shared interests with those who are not my own, and to collaborate with them to achieve shared ends. At worst, I recognize no shared interests and am disinclined to work toward the common good. Creating the best kinds of political arrangements is always a challenge because our inclination to collaborate works *both* toward upholding democratic (in the Deweyan sense) arrangements *and* toward undermining them.

An alternative title for this book might have been Solidarity. Or, if it didn't rub me and many others the wrong way, its gendered variant, Fraternity—a word still emblazoned on public school buildings in France as a political ideal having equal standing with Liberty and Equality. The book is titled "Collaboration" instead because of collaboration's buzzword status and also its Janus-faced connotations. Collaboration, unlike solidarity, is a contranym, a word that conveys a meaning and its opposite. To collaborate: to work with one's peers for mutual benefit. To collaborate: to sell out one's peers for personal gain. Whatever one calls it, this necessary third partner to liberty and equality—that much the French political trinity gets right—has always been a tricky ideal for pluralistic democracies. Throughout modern history, its achievement has often come at the expense of other ideals. Calls for fraternity, which seemed for a while a productive appeal to citizens to work together, always carried problematic connotations of ties by blood and gender, which have been perhaps the most powerful countervailing forces against liberty and equality in modern democracies. And the problem goes well beyond language. The moments when solidarity has been most in evidence have also been historical moments when religious/ethnic/racial pluralism and women's rights were suppressed. Workers' solidarity was strongest before unions were required to end long-term practices of race- and sex-based discrimination. National unity has always been easiest to mobilize when an enemy can be identified, as in World Wars, in the Cold War, and in the War on Terror. Unity so achieved is always to the detriment of those caught up in the dragnet of hostility—German speaking immigrants, Japanese Americans, Jews, "Socialists," Muslims. The Anglo-American strand of political philosophy has thus been understandably inclined to sideline this ideal, focusing on liberty and equality instead.

And yet, societies cannot function without the mutual commitment of citizens to one another. Call it the wholly spirit. Tricky though it is, it needs to take its place alongside liberty and equality because, as Benjamin Franklin reportedly said, if we don't hang together, we shall all hang separately.[15]

Thus, Dewey's insight that free and full communications with *other* social groups is the hallmark of a true democracy stands in uneasy tension with his insight that democracy *also* requires citizens' recognition of a *shared* problem and a commitment to solving it *together*. In exploring ways this tension plays out in schools, this book aims to, in Dewey's words, "extract the desirable traits of forms of community life which actually exist, and employ them to criticize undesirable features and suggest improvement."

How This Book Proceeds

This book moves from light, through darkness, and back into light. It begins with friendship, surely one of the most desirable traits of community life which actually exists. Not only are personal friendships invaluable, philosophers since Aristotle have noticed that something like friendship characterizes relations among community members that are rooted in reciprocal goodwill. "Friendship seems also to hold cities together, and lawgivers to care more about it than about justice," says Aristotle, "for concord seems to be something like justice, and this is what they aim at most of all, while taking special pains to eliminate civil conflict as something hostile."[16] It is unsurprising, therefore, that teachers will sometimes address a class as "friends" (as in "friends, it's time to pull out our pencils"), which makes a repeated pitch for concord as the group goes about its daily activities. This appellation becomes harder to pull off in older grades, as children's friendships become more enduring, more exclusive, and more central to children's growing sense of identity. Friendship, after all, implies a special fidelity, a selective commitment, which contrasts with the kind of goodwill you might show the rest of your peers—who are friends in a very loose sense perhaps, but not the same *kind* of friends. There is, to be sure, an enormous overlap between concord and personal friendship, and in the best societies the friendships that make us who we are and make our lives meaningful can be lived out in an environment marked not just by the absence of civil conflict but by the active and recognized presence of widespread mutual goodwill. These friendly relations among members of a community can be called "civic friendship" and they are, as Aristotle's lawgivers recognized, an essential basis of political life. The diminishment of civic friendship in many contemporary democracies, in which politically divided citizens view one another more as enemies than as friends who happen to disagree, is reason for alarm. Yet, as the skepticism of adolescents toward the idea that "we are all friends here" suggests, it won't do simply to say "let's all be friends."

The conflicting tugs of fidelity to personal friends and consent to the demands of authorities who represent the collective's wider interests (which sometimes conflict with the immediate interests of one's closest own) is the subject of Chapter 2. The chapter's analysis of friendship differs in focus from accounts that showcase friendship's glories and its rewards. The chapter does discuss several such accounts, namely Aristotle's and Montaigne's, but it attends especially to the tension between personal ties and the good of the group, especially that collective good as represented by authorities who act on the community's behalf (or claim to). This is, in fact, a subtext of Montaigne's essay, as the chapter explores. When fidelity to my personal friends is at odds with the public commitments expected of me by wider collectivities—by states, for instance, or political movements, or more abstractly by religious and moral principles and by the law—what am I to do? Although educators aspire to make schools friendly places, many children (perhaps all children at some point or another) experience them as sites of constraint and face this question. To children's navigation of that dilemma in schools, as portrayed in *Mindenki*, in the *Harry Potter* novels, and as described by real children, this chapter connects philosophical takes on the tension between a community's shared commitments, expressed through its political life, and personal friendships.

Chapter 3 turns to the dark side of collaboration. While portrayals of children standing up for their friends and for what's right make for charming novels and films, the sad truth is that people haven't always acted so admirably, nor has good always prevailed over evil. The word "collaborator" picked up its sense of traitorous assistance to enemy authority during and after Nazi occupations and the establishment of quisling governments, an episode in which collaboration's dark side was unavoidable. Unsurprisingly, in that war's wake philosophers took up questions it raised about citizens' responsibilities in situations of relative disempowerment, questions of what we owe others when it is hard and even dangerous to do the right thing. The conversation began immediately after the Second World War, with German philosopher Karl Jaspers's *The Question of German Guilt*, and it was continued by Hannah Arendt and others as a discussion of "collective responsibility." Later thinkers, especially Iris Marion Young, developed powerful insights into how the fact that our social, economic, and political lives involve working together creates a collective responsibility for justice, even as political and social structures incline us to collaborate in the worst sense, or at least produce pernicious effects unless we take pains to counteract them. Power is at the heart of the problem, and the chapter addresses that as well, especially as it plays out in schools.

Each of the thinkers discussed in Chapters 2 and 3 wrote in response to a perennial problem: how can groups of people find ways of working together that achieve their collective aims, their shared good, in the face of countervailing pulls toward discord? From Aristotle in ancient Athens to Iris Marion Young in the globalized twenty-first century, each was aware that the threats their social orders faced came as much from the inside of their societies as from the outside. That is as true now as ever. Our ability to keep on working together in societies hospitable to friendship, egalitarian in their power dynamics, and conscious of the responsibilities they generate among persons and toward the earth, relies on the conscious, deliberate cultivation of good collaborators in the best sense. The final chapter addresses the cultivation of two dimensions of togetherness that make collaborations sweet: consent and collegiality.

Children are asked to collaborate in schools, presumably in order to educate them to work together as adults, in a variety of ways. Not all in-school collaborations encourage children to treat one another as equals, nor do they all foster mutual commitment and responsibility. Very few give children genuine agency over the selection of their activity's aims. We allow children to choose which book to read for an assignment, but not to choose whether to read books, or for that matter complete any assignments whatsoever. (And not without reason! But the children aren't fooled into thinking they have agency, nor should adults be.) While it would be a grave mistake to *discourage* collaboration—if we don't hang together, we shall all hang separately, for sure—this book challenges the frequently heard, rarely questioned, blanket approval of *all* modes of collaboration, as if collaboration only ever went right, in order to draw educators' attention to the demanding ethical and political challenges of working together. My hope is that the better kinds of collaborative projects will be more regularly built into schooling, the more trivial recognized as merely trivial. The risk of celebrating the trivial, I suspect, is that it can mask those evils that take banal form—not incidentally, a guise that Hannah Arendt recognized and named in an account of war crimes that is very much an account of collaboration.

Chapters 3 and 4 offer examples of both kinds of collaboration in educational activities—the trivial in Chapter 3 via a discussion of "groupwork," and the ideal in Chapter 4. Chapter 4 presents the Village program, an extracurricular project designed by progressive educators, as an example of children's collaboration that involves agency, mutual responsibility, and the kind of fellow feeling that positive collaborations depend on. It is both a terrific program and impossible to replicate at the scale mass schooling demands. Its successes, however, are echoed in other kinds of collaborative projects that already happen in schools and that deserve more of our respect and financial support than they tend to get. Orchestras, theater performances, sports teams, student newspapers, and comparable activities offer students the opportunity to work with others toward ends they genuinely share. They cultivate a sense of mutual responsibility, as well as an understanding of one's agency and the responsibilities its use creates. Playing second chair clarinet, serving as the assistant director of the fall play, putting together the sports page for the school newspaper—these are collaborations that have the potential to prepare children for lifetimes of working together. They should be a well-resourced feature of any democracy's schools.

CHAPTER TWO

Friendship and Loyalty

Schools subject children to conflicting expectations. Comply with adults too eagerly and you find yourself derided as a goody-goody. Resist adult authority too staunchly, and you land yourself in detention. Schools are complicated social landscapes to navigate: there are rules, made by adults who claim always to be acting in children's best interests, interests that are not always identical with what children themselves perceive to be in their best interests. Fellow students are allies, or maybe rivals, or both, and are also figuring it all out themselves, sometimes with the help of older siblings and neighborhood friends, who might or might not be reliable. (Think of the words of "wisdom" you got from childhood peers on subjects like mean teachers, the transmission of cooties, and whichever urban legends were circulating in your time and place. To ignore peer knowledge was to risk disaster; to trust it, the same.) Childhood friendships can be made and broken in a matter of weeks, or months. Some last a lifetime. Strict teachers might turn out to be your strongest supporters, or they might humiliate you. Learning how to work with others in the complicated social landscape of school requires children to figure out how to balance and express commitments that are often incompatible. To begin with, students need to make friends.

Given the importance of friendship, it is unsurprising that almost all children's stories that win the hearts of readers provide perceptive depictions of such relationships. In some, friendships with peers are central. In others, readers might classify the central relationships as technically kinship bonds or human – animal bonds, but those relationships have the same place in the child's life as, and can reasonably be called, friendships. While any number of stories illustrate friendship's dynamics, J.K. Rowling's Harry Potter novels lend themselves especially well to this chapter's exploration of friendship as both the educative wellspring of collaborative impulses *and* a relationship that potentially creates conflicts with wider loyalties. For one, the novels depict children's friendships in the context of a school. Secondly, that school is set in a world of stark social and political conflict.[1] The fantastical setting permits moral clarity, whereas novels set in real political worlds have to leave ongoing conflicts more open-ended and unresolved. At the same time, Harry's close personal friendships with Ron and Hermione, his more casual friendships with other recurring characters in the books, and his antagonistic relationships with schoolmates whose families betrayed their peers to gain favor with the evil wizard Voldemort all offer compelling portrayals of how children learn to navigate ethical and political commitments through their relationships in schools, as well as how those commitments fit within a larger world of affiliations and disaffiliations that children are, over the course of their years in school, coming to understand. In recognizing friendship's relevance to politics, Rowling's depictions echo major philosophical accounts of friendship. More explicitly than most philosophical accounts, the novels also take up friendship's opposites, from mild distaste to flat out enmity. In doing so, the books raise questions about friendship and loyalty that children, like adults, puzzle over.

Those questions are the subject of this chapter. Who counts as a friend? If loyalty to a friend conflicts with other important loyalties—to authorities or an institution, to rules, to ideals, to other peers—how should we decide which loyalties to uphold?[2] What should we do if any of the entities to whom or which we owe loyalty turns out to be in the wrong? This chapter begins with canonical accounts of friendship by Montaigne and Aristotle and then turns to two modern accounts of personal relationships, one written just before the First World War and the other just before the Second. Significantly, each of these texts was written in the context of social and political friction, or in Aristotle's phrase "civil conflict," suggesting that personal affiliations beg for an account precisely when public affiliations are most fraught. Montaigne's essay *Of Friendship* was written during the French Wars of Religion, when the French, Catholic regime under which he lived was violently upheld and violently contested, and it subtly addresses tensions between his fidelity to his friend Étienne de la Boétie and his commitment to the value of social order. Montaigne's resolution, a separation of private from public life, certainly seems a reasonable response to civil war, but it sidesteps the problem of more generalized solidarity, no doubt because such solidarity was out of reach. If extended to include women and non-elites, it was also inconceivable to a man like Montaigne. Living in democracies that are closer to contemporary political arrangements, American philosopher Josiah Royce and British novelist E. M. Forster each sought justifiable grounds on which private and public loyalties could rest compatibly in liberal democracies. Royce wrote about loyalty just before the First World War, a moment of intense jingoism, impending war, class conflict, racist repression, and xenophobia. Forster published "What I Believe" in 1939, in the face of yet again all of the above. While conscious of flaws in the actual democracies they lived in, Royce and Forster each express a commitment to upholding democratic systems of governance, however imperfect. Whether or not these philosophical texts answer all of the above questions to readers' satisfaction, their insights into friendship and political obligation are fundamental to any effort to encourage the better kinds of collaboration while discouraging the worse.

Friendships and the Fantastic

Harry Potter and Ron Weasley are friends almost from the moment they meet, at age eleven. Not long after he hears the startling news that he is a wizard with a spot at the Hogwarts School of Witchcraft and Wizardry, Harry finds himself on the platform at King's Cross station, ticket to Hogwarts in hand but unsure how to find platform 9 ¾. He feels a rising panic until he observes the Weasley family's noisy, affectionate passage from London into the magical realm of the Hogwarts Express platform. He follows their lead. Ron's twin brothers Fred and George recognize Harry, thanks to the lightning shaped scar blazoned on his forehead left by Voldemort's attempt to kill him. The conversation that Harry overhears when Fred and George excitedly report back to the rest of the Weasley family tips Harry off to the fact that his fame among witches and wizards precedes him, and it also offers a hint as to where the Weasleys' loyalties lie. Harry and Ron share a train compartment, and over the course of the ride they share chocolate frogs, pumpkin pasties, and their new-school worries. Harry is alone with a pocket full of gold and silver coins. Ron has five older brothers and a second-hand rat. Each is anxious about measuring up, Harry to the new demands of wizardry and Ron to his family's record of success. As they contentedly snack, look out the window, and swap wizard cards, a friendship takes root. By the time fellow new-student Draco Malfoy enters the compartment and snobbishly advises Harry not to go making friends with the "wrong sort," Harry's loyalties are solidly with Ron. There they remain for the rest of the novels.[3]

In his essay *Of Friendship,* Michel de Montaigne describes meeting his friend Étienne de La Boétie under similar circumstances. When the two meet, each knows something about where the other is situated within a web of social relationships, and they hit it off from the start. "We sought each other before we met because of the reports we heard of each other, which had more effect on our affections than such reports would reasonably have," writes Montaigne. "We embraced each other by our names. And at our first meeting ... we found ourselves so taken with each other, so well acquainted, so bound together, that from that time on nothing was so close to us as each other."[4] In addition to compatibility and shared affiliations, reciprocal beneficence is at the core of both friendships. If, in a genuine friendship "one could give to the other, it would be the one who received the benefit who would oblige his friend," Montaigne says. "For, each of them seeking above all things to benefit the other, the one who provides the matter and the occasion is the liberal one, giving his friend the satisfaction of doing for him what he most wants to do."[5] From snacks to social connections, friends share, and they share for the satisfaction of meeting the other's wants and needs—felt almost as if they were one's own—rather than as a calculative *quid pro quo*.

Classic accounts of friendship by Aristotle and Cicero, both cited by Montaigne, define friendship along lines that, for all the abstraction of their language, provide a framework for understanding the children's friendships introduced so far (Harry's with Ron, Zsófia's with Liza), as well as Montaigne's with La Boétie, and probably yours with your best friend. Friends, according to Aristotle, each wish the friend's good for the friend's own sake, and both are aware that this well-wishing is mutual. In these classic accounts, reciprocal respect on the basis of the other's character is another defining feature of the best kind of friendship.[6] These character-based friendships are the kind contemporary speakers of English call personal friendships, or just friendships, as distinct from looser friendly ties like collegiality and acquaintance, or from kinship. Aristotle considered all of the above categorizable as *philia*, relationships involving a kind of love distinct from *eros*, or erotic love. If the relationship contained mutual, recognized, benevolence and was based on the moderate, non-erotic love (what we might call affection) of *philia*, it fell into the category

of relationship Aristotle thought to be a necessary piece of a
flourishing human life. After all, "nobody would choose to
live without friends even if he had all the other good things."[7]
What, Aristotle asks, would be the point of health, wealth, and
power if there were no one to share the goodness of one's life
with, no one to use it *for*?

Importantly, there were, for Aristotle, other possible and
legitimate bases for friendship than character, namely utility
and pleasure, in which the basis was either the friends' ongoing
usefulness to one another, or the pleasure the friends took in
shared activities. Think work colleagues, or neighbors, or the
pals you'd get together with for a bike ride or a card game,
friends who would send a meal over if you'd had surgery but
who wouldn't necessarily be privy to your most intimate needs
and concerns. More loosely still, pleasure and utility friends
could include the local bartender or barista who recognizes
you as a regular, parents you sometimes run into at your child's
school, that guy in the IT office. You wouldn't send them a meal
after surgery, but if you heard they'd had surgery you'd feel
a genuine pang of sympathy. You wish them well, as distinct
individuals (which distinguishes *philia* from generalized
compassion), and they wish you well in return. Aristotle calls
those very loose but wide-reaching ties "civic friendships,"
and they are an important basis of social and political life—
the basis of the kind of collaboration societies depend on. In
brief, friendships based on utility and pleasure are, though
less perfect than character friendships, still friendships. In
Aristotle's view, and in subsequent philosophical treatments
of friendship that use Aristotle's insights as a springboard, *all*
friendly relationships share the defining features of mutually
recognized well-wishing.

What makes Montaigne's account of friendship different
from Aristotle's, and more recognizable to modern readers
as a friendship (or, perhaps, makes it a recognizably
modern friendship) is its appreciation of the uniqueness
and serendipity of our most important friendships. With
Montaigne's essay, philosophy starts to treat friendship as

personal. In contrast to Aristotle, who portrays friends as generic exemplars of human virtue, Montaigne names his friend. He describes the particular time and place in which he and La Boétie met, the events that transpired, and the irreplaceability of his friend after his death. He writes in the first person; he conveys what the experience was *to him* of having, and being, a friend. For Montaigne, there can be no purely schematic account of why anyone becomes friends. "If you press me to tell why I loved him, I feel that this cannot be expressed, except by answering: Because it was he, because it was I."[8]

That sentiment is instantly recognizable. The first paragraphs of the essay, however, can throw readers for a loop because they seem to have nothing to do with friendship. *Of Friendship* introduces its author as proceeding like a painter, who "chooses the best spot, the middle of each wall, to put a picture labored over with all his skill, and the empty space all around it he fills with grotesques, which are fantastic paintings whose only charm lies in their variety and strangeness."[9] *Of Friendship* is typically printed smack in the middle of Montaigne's *Essays*, after essays on subjects as varied as *Whether the Governor of a Besieged Place Should Go Out to Parley, Of Fear* and *Of Custom,* and before essays such as *Of Cannibals, Of War Horses* and *Of Smells.* Asking presumably of his other essays, Montaigne wonders "And what are these things of mine but grotesques and monstrous bodies, pieced together of divers members, without definite shape, having no order, sequence, or proportion other than accidental?"[10] Further confusing matters, the picture-at-the-center that Montaigne promises is whisked away before it appears. What Montaigne initially says he will center is a text not about but *by* La Boétie: *Discourse on Voluntary Servitude.* Continuing the wall-painting analogy, Montaigne says he will print La Boétie's piece at the center of his own writing because "my ability does not go far enough for me to dare to undertake a rich, polished picture, formed according to art. It has occurred to me to borrow one from Étienne de La Boétie, which will do honor to all the rest of this work."[11] By the essay's conclusion, however, Montaigne has changed course.

> Because I have found that [*Voluntary Servitude*] has since been brought to light, and with evil intent, by those who seek to disturb and change the state of our government without worrying whether they will improve it, and because they have mixed his work up with some of their own concoctions, I have changed my mind about putting it in here.[12]

At the center of the book, the reader is left instead with *Of Friendship*.

The reader might well wonder what a text that lends itself to being mobilized to "disturb and change the state of government" had to do with friendship anyway! And, since it was left out, why mention it at all? Does its mention at the beginning and end of an essay that instead puts La Boétie's friendship with Montaigne, or at least Montaigne's account of it, at the center make La Boétie's written discourse another fantastic grotesque ("mixed up" as it was with other "concoctions") framing the ideal? Or does the absence of that "rich polished picture" mean that personal friendship itself turns out to be just one more body "pieced together of divers members, without definite shape, having no order, sequence or proportion other than accidental"?[13]

As his decision to leave out the text of *Voluntary Servitude* acknowledges, Montaigne's friendship with La Boétie was set against the backdrop of impending civil war. These are friends who had to choose and maintain their loyalties carefully, as their loyalties had political as well as personal consequences. In spite of Montaigne's statement that "there was I know not what inexplicable and fateful force that was the mediator of this union," he and La Boétie met when both were young men striving for professional success in the small world of the sixteenth-century Bordeaux judiciary.[14] Extensive family connections linked them, and with La Boétie, who was a few years older than Montaigne, having already made a name for himself as an exceptional orator and promising writer, Montaigne stood to gain professionally from the friendship.[15] They embraced each other by their names because those names meant something. None of that undermines Montaigne's claim to have loved his friend; rather, it is a reminder that friendships always unfold amidst other social, political, and personal ties and aspirations. In settings like the French Southwest at the outset of the French Wars of Religion (1562–1598), the personal ties of a member of the provincial elite had potentially life-or-death implications. Approximately 3 million people are estimated to have died in those wars as Protestants and Catholics battled for prominence. Elite families affiliated themselves with one side or the other in battles that were as much about power as faith. Montaigne himself spent part of 1588 jailed in Paris, after which he retired from political life to write.

Read with this context in mind, *Of Friendship* raises questions about potentially conflicting tugs of loyalty that are of enduring relevance. La Boétie died (likely from dysentery) in 1563, just as the conflict was heating up. Montaigne was at his friend's deathbed, where "La Boétie placed Montaigne before a series of responsibilities that were later to haunt him. Whether it was by bequeathing his library to him or by begging him to see in his friend a 'brother' and continue a work originally conceived to be written together, La Boétie assigned to Montaigne a political mission with far-reaching implications."[16] *Of Friendship* mentions two pieces of La Boétie's writing in its first paragraphs. The more significant of those, *Voluntary Servitude*, written in 1546 or 1548 and continuing to circulate in manuscript form after La Boétie's death, raises questions about freedom and obedience to state authority. La Boétie's second manuscript was a concrete policy proposal, less theoretical but also a problem for Montaigne because it expressed ideas that both the Protestant and Catholic sides had, by the time he was publishing his *Essays*, firmly opposed. It is now mainly a historical curiosity.

Voluntary Servitude, however, explores questions that continue to hold broad interest: how persons are conditioned to submit to the authority of rulers, how the psychology of self-subjugation upholds autocrats, and how one might maintain some freedom by separating one's personal from one's political self.

Why, La Boétie asks, have human beings, the only creatures with a natural right to freedom, surrendered that freedom to political rulers? Unlike Thomas Hobbes, John Locke, Jean-Jacques Rousseau, and others who asked versions of that same question and then puzzled over the legitimacy of any political order based on such surrender, La Boétie stuck mostly to its psychological dimension. *Why* would human beings give up their freedom? The answer, for La Boétie, lies in the human inclination to make friends.

Collaboration at its best and worst is at the core of La Boétie's discourse. Like later social contract theorists, La Boétie believed that we are naturally free and equal and that rulers gain their power through our consent to state authority. Unlike Hobbes (who thought relations among free persons naturally tended to hostility), Locke (who thought humans naturally assembled into families), and Rousseau (who thought free humans were naturally indifferent to one another), La Boétie supposes that human beings are naturally inclined to *friendship*. He takes it as "clear and evident," that "nature has created us, and formed us in the same mold, to show us that we are all equals, or rather brothers."[17] (As in most social contract theories and most philosophical accounts of friendship, women are not included, except insofar as feminized "nature" serves as the "good mother" who sets men up for liberty, equality, and fraternity.[18]) Fraternity here is a matter of not only sentiment but also an impulse to mutual aid. Nature did not make some men more clever than others, some stronger than others in order to set them up in a field of battle or turn them into brigands, says La Boétie. Instead, nature created differences "to cause fraternal affections to be born in men, and to make them put those into practice because some are able to provide help and others are in need of it."[19] Men are formed by nature to "recognize oneself in another as if in a mirror," a phrase that (no doubt deliberately) echoes Aristotle's description of friends as like mirrors to one another. Because nature made men for "the communication and exchange of our thoughts, the communion of our wills; because she has searched for all possible means to make and strengthen the knot of our alliance," La Boétie asks, "how can we doubt that we are naturally free, because we are naturally equals?"[20] *We are made to be free because we are made to be friends.* "We are made," La Boétie says, "such that the mutual obligations of friendship take up a good part of our lives."[21]

Tragically, man's penchant for friendly affiliation also drives his self-subjugation to tyrants. Because we are naturally inclined to friendship, it seems reasonable to "love virtue, to honor noble deeds, to appreciate goods received, and to reduce our own well-being for the sake of honoring and bringing advantage to someone who loves us and who deserves to be loved." This, however, can go very wrong. Once rulers get a foot in the door, they gain the means to provide and withhold good things, and they will not necessarily continue to act in the interests of those they formerly treated as equals. Furthermore, they are often succeeded by heirs or cronies who lack their virtues. What interests La Boétie most, though, is not what motivates rulers but instead what motivates those who prop up tyrants even when they stand to gain more by insisting on equality. As he points out, there's a conundrum here: all it would take to topple any tyrant would be for people to stop propping the tyrant up. Sometimes, of course, this happens, and La Boétie's book is an important text in the philosophical literature on civil disobedience. What usually forestalls liberation, La Boétie argues, is a combination of factors. The people (by which La Boétie means something like "the masses," or the common folk) are bought off by bread and circus: by holidays, handouts, spectacle. Over time, they become so accustomed to subservience that they forget the freedom and equality that should have been theirs.

But the real "source and secret of domination, the basis and foundation of tyranny" is the willingness of a few persons to band together to prop up the tyrant. A small handful realize they can gain power and material gain for themselves through collaboration. Hierarchies of patronage form. Sixty answer to the six who uphold the one, says La Boétie; six hundred to the sixty, six thousand to the six hundred, with the individuals at each level seeing only the advantages of placing themselves over those below. This is collaboration in its worst sense, and it eliminates the very remembrance of freedom and equality. It also eliminates the possibility of genuine friendship because friendship "blossoms in equality."[22] *Voluntary Servitude* turns out to be a serious contender for the picture of friendship at the center of Montaigne's wall after all.

Voluntary Servitude was picked up by Calvinists in Geneva, who republished portions to bolster their arguments against church and royal authority over individual conscience. Although La Boétie was a staunch Catholic, his discourse naturally lent itself to the Protestant cause.[23] Montaigne's association with the text and its writer thus became a liability. He had made a deathbed promise of brotherhood and literary collaboration to his friend La Boétie, who in his last delirious moments had asked Montaigne to save him "a place." Montaigne had promised he would. Yet to publicly celebrate the man and his work could put Montaigne's own life and liberty at risk. Montaigne's account of his friendship with La Boétie in *Of Friendship* carefully describes both the friendship and La Boétie's writing in terms that downplay any potential threat to the social order, while also keeping an awareness of La Boétie's work in circulation. In a dangerous world, Montaigne hedges his bets. He retreats from public life into his library to write about the fantastic friendship he lost, a friendship "so entire and so perfect that certainly you will hardly read of the like, and among men of today you see no trace of it in practice."[24] From that library, he points readers to the ideas of La Boétie's that he could not, himself, publish.

Loyalty and Snitching

Other friendships in the Harry Potter novels are formed in less idealized "because it was he, because it was I" circumstances, and they present more complicated instances of children negotiating conflicting loyalties at school—a situation from which they generally have no good possibility of retreat (though libraries remain a solid option). Ron and Harry eventually become friends with Hermione Granger, after she makes an unfavorable first impression. One fall day, Hermione, a classic know-it-all, gets on Ron's nerves when she corrects his pronunciation of a spell he can't pull off. "It's no wonder no one can stand her," Ron comments to Harry after class, and Hermione, having overheard, runs off in tears. Everything changes that evening, when Harry and Ron realize that Hermione is still crying in the bathroom even as an angry troll is roaming the school corridors. They disobey their teachers' orders to return to their rooms, seek out Hermione, and together the three fell the troll when it corners them in the bathroom. Impressive though this collaborative problem solving is, it leaves Ron and Harry in serious trouble with their teachers. What clinches the threesome's friendship is Hermione's willingness to take full blame for Ron and Harry's contravention of the teachers' order to go to their dormitories. Although her credibility with teachers was such that she could easily have escaped their wrath when they found the three students with the unconscious troll, Hermione concocts a quick fib that it was her idea to stop the troll and that Harry and Ron had stepped in to save her from her own foolishness. After that, the three are friends.

If Hermione's willingness to lie to teachers out of loyalty to her classmates proves to Ron and Harry that she is worthy of their friendship, Neville's refusal to do so also renders him worthy of their respect. At the climax of the first novel, the trio of friends plans to sneak out of their rooms at night to interfere with Voldemort's plot to steal a magical stone that conveys immortality. Neville tries to block the door, and when Ron tells him to "get away ... and don't be an idiot," he refuses. "Don't you call me an idiot," Neville exclaims. "I don't think you should be breaking any more rules! And you were the one who told me to stand up to people!" "Yes," says Ron with exasperation, "but not to *us!*"[25] Hermione temporarily paralyzes Neville with a spell, and Harry, Ron, and Hermione do succeed in saving the stone, but at the final dinner that wraps up the school year, school headmaster Dumbledore recognizes Neville's valor as well as theirs. "There are all kinds of courage," he tells the assembled students. "It takes a great deal of bravery to stand up to our enemies, but just as much to stand up to our friends."[26] From this point on, Neville is also a valued friend and ally.

In schools where the choices aren't as stark as civil war or the ultimate battle of good versus evil, children still find themselves needing to figure out how to negotiate conflicting obligations. When is it more important to stand by one's friends; when is the right choice upholding the rules? A nine-year-old once shared with me her uncertainty about how to respond to a friend's actions when she was asked to accompany him to the main office on an errand. On the way back from the office, he stopped to look into another child's unlocked locker for any Pokémon cards to steal. She knew this was wrong, but she wasn't sure what to do about it. "The teachers tell us that we should talk to them if someone does something that makes us uncomfortable," she explained, "but he's my friend, and if I tell the teacher on him, he'll get in big trouble and not want to be my friend anymore." Adults may have answers to offer—that theft is wrong and therefore telling a teacher is the right thing to do, for instance, or that she should think about how the person whose cards were being stolen might feel, or that she should have confronted her friend directly. The point, though, is that children need to learn to figure out answers for themselves. As they figure them out, few tags are more disgraceful than "snitch." The fact that advice columns are chock full of questions about how to respond when a work colleague, family member, or friend does something one considers unethical suggests that such conundrums of divided loyalty continue to matter, and their answers continue to seem not at all straightforward to adults. Decontextualized admonishments to "be accountable" are of little use. Accountable to what, or to whom? That's the hard question.

Classic philosophical accounts of friendship are of limited use in resolving this kind of practical conundrum because for Plato, Aristotle, Cicero, and Montaigne, there can be no serious conflict between friendship and ethical obligations. True friends are, by definition, united in their virtuous convictions.[27] No true friend would make the wrong judgment about whether or not to sneak around and take things that weren't his because if he did, by definition he wouldn't be a true friend—which is, perhaps, why Montaigne took friendship to be exceedingly rare. By the twentieth century, friendship had to be squared differently with other ethical and political obligations. Josiah Royce and E.M. Forster, each writing on the brink of world war and in the face of intensifying nationalist, populist, and partisan politics, offer accounts of friendship that acknowledge the imperfect virtue of friends as well as governments. Both uphold the value of personal friendships, though in a less idealized form than Montaigne's or Aristotle's, and like La Boétie they treat friendship as of a piece with an egalitarian social contract, which they call democracy. Importantly, both leave room for friendships and democracies that are other than perfect but are mutually supportive. Friendship reinforces democracy, and democracy reinforces friendship—because both friendships and democracies are understood as long-term, egalitarian, collaborative relationships.

Loyalty is a virtue at the heart of friendship (and political systems) that raises a host of problems, as all the examples above suggest. Without some degree of loyalty, there can be no trust, but loyalty is also the root of corruption, factionalism, and authoritarianism. Loyalty can therefore seem to be merely a motivational spur, good only insofar as the ends it serves are good. Josiah Royce, however, makes the case that loyalty is essentially, not just conditionally, good, or in other words good in and of itself. In fact, Royce says, it is *the* primary virtue. "In loyalty," he contends, "when loyalty is properly defined, is the fulfilment of the whole moral law. You can truthfully centre your entire moral world about a rational conception of loyalty."[28] This is a bold claim. Royce's argument hinges on how he defines loyalty, as well as each of the terms that definition contains. For Royce, loyalty is "*[t]he willing and practical and thoroughgoing devotion of a person to a cause. A man is loyal when, first, he has some cause* to which he is loyal; when, secondly, he *willingly* and *thoroughly* devotes himself to this cause; and when, thirdly, he expresses his devotion in some *sustained and practical way.*"[29]

Loyalty, says Royce, is good because it makes possible the constitution of a coherent self. How loyalty constitutes selfhood rests on Royce's conception of a *cause*. Whether the cause be good or bad, Royce says, it must have two features as an object of loyalty. "If one is loyal, he has a cause which he indeed personally values …. He therefore takes interest in the cause, loves it, is well pleased with it."[30] It must, that is, be valued by the loyal person himself, not merely presented by others as an appropriate object of allegiance.

> On the other hand, loyalty never means the mere emotion of love for your cause, and never means merely following your own pleasure, viewed *as* your private pleasure and interest. For if you are loyal, your cause is viewed by you as something outside of you. Or if, like your country, your cause includes yourself, it is still much larger than your private self. It has its own value, so you as a loyal person believe.[31]

For Royce, that is, loyalty is importantly and invariably *social* as well as personal. What loyalty to a cause offers, regardless of the cause's merits, is the possibility of ordering otherwise incoherent preferences and inclinations into a plan of life. Looking only to what one wants from moment to moment,

Royce points out, a person would be pulled in all directions, unable to choose among desires. Devotion to a cause gives a person grounds for choosing one direction over another, grounds that are personally relevant yet never merely private.

Royce considers and rejects several other accounts of loyalty, and of individual and society, which he associates with particular interlocutors. His counter arguments further illuminate his reasons for considering loyalty the primary virtue. A "young Russian friend," he says (in the waning days of Czarist rule), raises the charge that loyalty is a virtue that upholds oppression. Its association with entrenched political regimes that launch wars and manipulate the masses sets it against justice. Royce's response is that loyalty *can* work in the interests of oppressors but will not *necessarily* do so. At best, it is employed by individuals using their own judgment and works on behalf of causes that benefit society at large. Royce's most extensive refutation goes to a cluster of objections that he calls "ethical individualism." He associates ethical individualism with Nietzsche but views it as expressed also in modern plays, newspapers, and novels—Nietzsche-lite, as it were. "The modern man – yes the modern woman also, as we sometimes are told – can be content only with the completest possible self-development and the fullest self-expression which the conditions of our social life permit."[32] Such self-development, however, can be found only through loyalty, argues Royce, because freedom of self-expression is useless without loyalty. Without loyalty there is simply nothing to express.

> You are autonomous of course. You can even cut loose from all loyalty if you will. I only plead that if you do so, if you wholly decline to devote yourself to any cause whatever, your assertion of moral independence will remain but an empty proclaiming of a moral sovereignty over your life, without any definite life over which to be sovereign. For the only definite life that you can live will be a social life. This social life may indeed be one of enmity to society. But in that case your social order will crush you ... Your last word

will then be simply the empty phrase 'Lo, I asserted myself.' But in the supposed case of your enmity to society, you will never know what it was that you thus asserted when you asserted yourself. *For a man's self has no contents, no plans, no purposes, except those which are, in one way or another, defined for him by his social relations.*[33]

For Royce, neither self nor society can take any shape without the other.

If this establishes that loyalty has value in itself, it has not yet addressed the problem of conflicts between what Royce calls causes. What if you are Montaigne, loyal to a Catholic royal order *and* to your commitment to keep your friend's work alive after his death? And what if, worse still, one or the other (or both!) of those causes is doing harmful things, like fomenting violent conflict? And don't *most* of the causes that celebrate loyalty tend to do that—all the various "closed" societies that Dewey worried about, gangs, armies, elites and so forth? *The Philosophy of Loyalty* counters these associations of loyalty with anti-democratic, anti-egalitarian, and often violent associations by calling for a transcendence of all provincial loyalties through "loyalty to loyalty." The loyal person, recognizing the importance of his own cause to himself, will ultimately appreciate the loyalty of others to their own causes, says Royce, even when those causes conflict with his own. Take, for instance, Ron, Harry, and Hermione gaining a new respect for Neville because he stood up for what he thought to be his classmates' best interests, and his own, and the right thing to do, even as he tried to thwart their immediate plans. In appreciating others' loyalty for its own sake, the loyal person appreciates others as capable of loyalty and will therefore strive to make possible their continuation of that loyalty. Remember that Royce understands loyalty as what integrates the otherwise-chaotic psyche into an agentic self. To appreciate another person's loyalty is to appreciate his or her human selfhood. In Royce's account, loyalty to loyalty is another way of saying loyalty to the value of human lives lived meaningfully. Loyalty to loyalty thus provides a response to the evils associated with unjust wars, xenophobia, and oppression—evils of which Royce was well aware.[34] Because such projects diminish someone else's opportunity to live a meaningful life, they must be rejected.[35]

Royce was an Idealist, confident that history was moving on a progressive trajectory. One world war later, with noxious demands for loyalty running strong in Stalinist left-wing and Fascist right-wing politics, and with idealism of all stripes looking like naivete, E.M. Forster also put his faith in political communities that upheld the possibility of friendly relations, but he expresses far more skepticism than Royce. "I do not believe in Belief," his 1939 essay "What I Believe" begins.

> But this is an age of faith, and there are so many militant creeds that, in self-defence, one has to formulate a creed of one's own. Tolerance, good temper, and sympathy are no longer enough in a world which is rent by religious and racial persecution, in a world where ignorance rules, and science, who ought to have ruled, plays the subservient pimp. Tolerance, good temper and sympathy – they are what matter really, and if the human race is not to collapse they must come to the front before long. But for the moment they are not enough, their action is no stronger than a flower, battered beneath a military jackboot. They want stiffening, even if the process coarsens them.[36]

Forster laments that he finds himself living in such an age of faith. "It is extremely unpleasant really. It is bloody in every sense of the word. And I have to keep my end up in it."[37] Forster hails Montaigne (alongside Erasmus) as his "law-giver," but unlike Montaigne he considers it impossible to separate one's private from one's public life. He has to keep his end up. "Where do I start?" asks Forster. "With personal relationships."[38]

Relationships, Forster says, are "comparatively solid in a world full of violence and cruelty" though "not absolutely solid." In the 1920s and 1930s, Freud's theories of the human mind had become widely known, and Forster recognizes that "[p]sychology has split and shattered the idea of a 'Person.'" Royce's earlier confidence that loyalty could unify and stabilize the self had become untenable. "[T]here is something incalculable in each of us," as Forster paraphrases Freud, "which may at any moment rise to the surface and destroy our normal balance. We don't know what we are like. We can't know what other people are like." How then is anyone to put his faith in personal relationships? "In theory," says Forster, "we cannot. But in practice we can and do."[39]

Forster turns to "love and loyalty" as he aims to "get a little order into the contemporary chaos."[40] His goals are modest. He doubts the promises of security made by personhood and creed, but he recognizes that "one must be fond of people and trust them if one is not to make a mess of life."[41] This brings Forster to a declaration that is easily misinterpreted if read out of context. "I hate the idea of causes," he says, "and *if I had to choose between betraying my country and betraying my friend I hope I should have the guts to betray my country*."[42] Forster seems to be with Hermione here; caught between obedience to rules, no matter how good those rules, and loyalty to friends, friends win. Yet as long as some citizens are able to retreat to libraries and others are not, this declaration lends itself to charges of political quietism, and even, on the brink of the Second World War, culpable obliviousness to the suffering of others. Forster doesn't end the essay with those words, though. "Probably one will not be asked to make such an agonizing choice," he says, but all the same "[l]ove and loyalty to an individual can run counter to the claims of the State. When they do – down with the State, say I, which means that the State would down me." There may be consequences, but any state that requires citizens to betray friends is not a state worthy of support. Importantly, not all states do require betrayals of friends, and those states *are* worthy of support.

Where Royce's hopes are soaring, Forster's are modest. Royce's aim is a "beautiful community" that will forestall future wars, while Forster's is "not to make a mess of life." Both, however, anchor their ethical commitment to others in a simultaneous commitment to political communities hospitable to friendships. While staking their faith in personal relationships and questioning the righteousness of the actual democratic states they lived in, Royce and Forster—like La Boétie—recognize an allowance for friendship as the critical difference between egalitarian, liberal states and tyrannical regimes. Royce's writing on the "beautiful community" was picked up by John Dewey and later by Martin Luther King Jr., each of whom developed the idea into a defense of democratic politics. Forster's essay appears in a collection called *Two Cheers for Democracy*, whose title comes from passages in "What I Believe." "Democracy is not a Beloved Republic really, and never will be," he says, but it deserves our support anyway. Democracy "does start from the assumption that the individual is important, and that all types are needed to make a civilisation."[43] It admits criticism. Hence, two cheers. Only love, says Forster, merits a third.

Fortunately, the conflicting obligations that come up in school generally put children in situations less fraught than battles against fascists or evil wizards. (There are commonalities though—grotesque drawings, militant creeds, even, in the age of Big Data, science playing the subservient pimp.) That said, schools are rife with the kinds of loyalty that Royce aimed to transcend, and schoolchildren regularly feel caught between the rock of friendship and the hard place of adults' expectations. Some conflicts are inevitable, even valuable. Only by making difficult choices, experiencing the consequences, and learning to maintain both personal and "civic" friendships in spaces like schools can children learn how to collaborate in its positive sense. Because the adults who are the authorities in children's lives have a hand in creating these conflicts, it behooves us to think carefully about what our expectations, the situations we set up, and the consequences for missteps motivate children to do. In the assignments teachers give, in their assessments of those assignments, and in the ways classroom time is structured, children can be encouraged to foster mutually supportive relationships in which one person's gain is also another's, or they can be encouraged to compete, to consider peers a drag or a resource to exploit. They can learn to work with peers or turn to those in power as a means of achieving their goals. While collective projects, including sports teams, drama, bands and orchestras, group projects, and more, provide the context for learning to be the best kind of collaborator, their mere existence is just the first step. It matters *how* children are encouraged to work together within them. Encouraging the kinds of friendships and loyalties that democracy both fosters and relies upon requires adults also to think deeply about how the terms of those collective projects motivate children to treat one another.

CHAPTER THREE

Responsibility and Power

Groupwork

Groupwork, meaning assignments designed to be completed collaboratively, evokes mixed feelings. Groupwork can be very short term, such as twenty-minute activities during a class session—a science lab, say, or an art project, or a small-group discussion. Groupwork can also involve longer-term, larger-scale assignments, like a science fair project, a music performance, or a collaborative presentation. Students find some of these collaborations richly rewarding; they find others exasperating, trivial, or guilt-inducing. At best, group projects highlight the different strengths of different people, create situations in which students can help each other grow, and foster so-called "soft skills" like listening and flexibility (which are in fact very hard skills). At worst, the workload is not divided fairly and students are left feeling exploited, frustrated, or sidelined—or the experience further confirms that one can coast through life on the labor of others. Structuring group projects carefully can forestall some of these effects, but pitfalls remain a constant hazard. Adults know this through the collaborations we ourselves are required to take part in. Who hasn't occasionally felt exploited, frustrated, or sidelined—or relieved at the chance to avoid heavy lifting—when a team effort was required at work or in a voluntary association?

At the same time, who hasn't felt a special kind of satisfaction when a collaborative project goes well?

Some experiences of collaboration, that is, are what John Dewey would call educative, while others are miseducative. Before examining the difference and what makes particular experiences of collaboration one or the other, consider Dewey's understanding of "experience." Any experience, Dewey contends, is marked by two criteria: continuity and interaction.[1] "Continuity" indicates that an individual's present experience is always continuous with her past and future experiences. While experiencing something in the present, each of us draws on what we have learned from past, relevantly similar, experiences and carries what we learn from the present experience into future experiences. Take, for instance, a group of students in a primary school science class assigned a collaborative presentation of the muscular system. In this instance of groupwork, they will draw on skills, habits, preferences developed through past experiences.[2] Different individuals may have leadership skills, or artistic abilities, or a love of science, or a dislike of the particular peers in the group. These fruits of past experience will *continue* into the present experience. If the upshot is a surprisingly satisfying collaboration, perhaps that dislike of peers will turn into friendlier relations that continue into the future. If the upshot is a frustrating and mediocre performance, that love of science may go forwards more weakly. Importantly, "there is some kind of continuity in any case since every experience affects for better or worse the attitudes which help decide the quality of further experiences, by setting up certain preference and aversion, and making it easier or harder to act for this or that end," says Dewey. "Moreover, every experience influences in some degree the objective conditions under which further experiences are had."[3] Continuity, therefore, "is involved … in every attempt to discriminate between experiences that are worthwhile educationally and those that are not."[4] If *continuity* captures the subjective, internal aspect of an experience, *interaction* captures the fact that any experience takes place in interaction with a particular environment, material, and also social. In creating that presentation of the muscular system, the students will interact with the materials provided, with the set up of the classroom or other workspaces, with one another, and with the teacher. The science textbook or art materials, for instance, will interact with students' learned ability and willingness to use them.

Experiences that are educative lead to growth, which is to say a further expansion and enrichment of experiences. A miseducative experience, in contrast, "has the effect of arresting or distorting the growth of further experience."[5] The student surprised to discover that her peers were more amiable than she expected has had, in this respect at least, an educative experience. The student who likes science a little less has had a miseducative one. It is possible, as these examples suggest, for a collaboration to be educative to one student and miseducative to another, or educative in some aspects and miseducative in others. Further complicating the matter, it is also possible that something that seems educative in the moment turns out not to be so. Students can improve their standardized test scores by taking test-prep courses. If the side effect of the experience is disenchantment with schooling, it has been a miseducative experience even if they ace the test. Parents can also improve their children's standardized test scores by shaping the public school system (insofar as they have the means)—by pressing schools to track students internally, by moving to a higher-performing and thus likely better-resourced district, by voting to take public funds out of the public system—in ways that maximize their children's ability to outscore other test-takers. As Dewey sees it, this is also miseducative. It involves a restriction of contacts, a limitation of connections, which shuts off opportunities to grow in new and unexpected directions. It limits free and full interplay with other forms of association. Dewey illustrates miseducative experiences that seem to involve growth but don't by using the example of a gang of thieves, who improve in thievery but whose contacts with the outside world are necessarily somewhat closed off. There is also an element of time in gaging the quality of an experience, as every experience has "an immediate aspect of agreeableness or disagreeableness" but also an "influence on later experiences." This, says Dewey, "sets a problem to the educator. It is his business to arrange for the kinds of experiences which, while they do not repel the student, but rather engage his activities are, nevertheless, more than immediately enjoyable since they promote having desirable future experiences."[6]

It might seem that teachers can easily design collaborative projects that are educative, rather than miseducative, by turning to evidence-based "best practices" that have been collected in lists available via a quick search on the internet. If that were so, this book could end right here. Examples include breaking down an assignment into clear tasks, structuring it so that students must draw on each other's different skills to complete the assignment, and explicitly teaching students ways to share ideas and resolve conflicts. These are useful guidelines. They are not in themselves adequate to ensure that collaborations are educative. Even the best list of best practices is insufficient because, in the sense philosophers give the word "practice," they are not really *practices* as all. They are techniques, which are only effective when used within a practice, by an adept practitioner. Hence, this chapter has more to say.

Starting with Aristotle, and continuing with considerable refinement and elaboration into the present, philosophers have distinguished what Aristotle called *techne*, which we might call "technical reason," from what he called *phronesis* and we call "practical reason," or judgment. Technical reason aims to establish "nomological knowledge: law-like explanations establishing correlations within the phenomenal field that hold reliably under conditions precisely specified in the laws. This knowledge then has predictive value: under conditions a, b, and c, it can be reliably predicted that x, y, and z will occur."[7] Technical reasoning was key to the scientific revolution, and it continues to be invaluable when it comes to matters like creating safe vaccines, designing stable bridges, and maintaining soil conditions for sustainable agriculture. Scientists and engineers tackling such problems take a detached, objective approach, thinking in terms of generalizable findings uncovered by means of standardized procedures. Experiments are run; numbers are crunched. As the adjectives in those sample projects—safe, stable, sustainable—suggest, however, projects properly addressed using technical reasoning are typically embedded in value-laden practices, in these cases medicine, engineering, and agriculture. Unlike the procedures and techniques they incorporate, *practices* cannot be understood without consideration of their ultimate, and always in part moral, ends.[8] Understanding what makes a vaccine "safe," for instance, requires an understanding of what medicine is *for,* and that is an ethical as well as technical matter. So-called "best practices" for collaborative projects can help educators set up conditions a, b, and c for achieving x, y, and z, but they offer no insight into whether adopting a, b, and c to achieve x, y, and z will be, in Dewey's language, *educative*. To determine that requires an understanding of collaboration's ethical dimensions that lists of best practices cannot capture.

In addition to consideration of the moral aims of the practice, practical reasoning involves a kind of know-how that cannot be encapsulated in rules. Unlike technical reasoning, practical reasoning requires a first-person knowledge that incorporates discernment of the particulars of the situation, appreciation of the aims of the endeavor, and familiarity with established norms and procedures applicable to cases like the one at hand.[9] In many practices, this knowledge is, at least to some degree, literally "at hand," incorporated in the sense of embodied. Examples would be a farmer who can tell by the feel of the soil whether a field needs water, a cook who can adjust seasonings to taste, or a seamstress who can tell by the feel of the fabric how it will drape when tailored into a garment. Such reasoning cannot be reduced to a set of general rules, which is not to say that there are no norms. Rather, the standards of good practice are applied by practitioners who have the knowledge to ascertain what the case requires, as well as the imagination and know how to apply rules flexibly, always with an eye to the aims of the practice.

Ultimately, practical reasoning involves judgment, which carries the uncertainty that comes with the variable, unpredictable reality of human action in the material world, as well as an inevitable weighting of the value of different possible outcomes. The success or failure of a practice always has something to do with how well its outcomes balance the good ends it aimed to achieve with alternative, even conflicting, ends. Sustainable agriculture is more expensive in the short term: how, then, to weigh the desirability of feeding people now against feeding people in the future? How safe is safe enough, when it comes to vaccines? These are unavoidably matters of judgment.

Education is a practice, and as such it requires practical reasoning. This is why best practices are useful but insufficient. They function like recipes for cooks: if you know how to cook, they can tell you a new way to do something, and if you don't know how to cook they can help you learn. What they cannot tell you is whether your judgment that you've cooked a dish well stands up to scrutiny, or whether what you think you want to eat is worth eating. In the case of a roast chicken or a marshmallow, the stakes are low. But when it comes to aims like figuring out a way to achieve the togetherness every society needs without jeopardizing liberty, individuality, and equality along the way, sophisticated practical reasoning—about both means and ends—is called for. The fact that collaboration can entail *either* working with peers to achieve shared interests for the sake of the common good *or* working with authorities in ways that undermine shared interests for the sake of one's own good—and that the former is essential to living amicably together, even as the latter lurks as a constant hazard—means that educators need judgment when it comes to collaborative activities, not just techniques.

Consider again Ms. Erika. In the beginning scenes of *Mindenki*, she led the chorus in an *effective* collaboration but not an educative one. The means she used (silencing less polished singers) were miseducative, in part because her ends (winning competitions while preserving a façade of inclusion) had overridden the intrinsically educational aims of teaching children to sing and fostering their love of music. Few educators aspire to emulate Ms. Erika. To some extent, her missteps can be avoided by teachers who reason carefully about what kinds of labor a particular collective project encourages, about how roles are established and held within the group, and about how children's appeals to adult authority are addressed. In exercising good judgment about these and other practical aspects of collaboration, two features of collaboration call for deeper consideration: mutual responsibility and power relations.[10] Ideally, responsibilities in schools will be consciously upheld, and power will be wielded in support of friendship as addressed in the last chapter rather than along lines that promote discord. To exercise a well-tuned practical reasoning in the classroom that matches that of an expert carpenter or cook, however, educators need a sophisticated appreciation of power's effects on collaboration, and the distorted shouldering of responsibility those effects can create.

Not to be forgotten is that Ms. Erika was herself working within a school system that no doubt expected *her* to be a good collaborator, to direct the chorus toward the achievement of objectives shared by other adults in the school community. Beyond that, the parents and administrators expecting Ms. Erika's chorus to be inclusive and to win were *themselves* under pressure to be good collaborators in even wider social projects—raising economically and socially successful children, for instance, and thereby helping build the new Hungary. The kinds of collaborative projects teachers design for schoolchildren cannot be separated from the collaborative projects that school systems expect, and even require, teachers themselves to engage in. Ms. Erika could have used better judgment, to be sure, but it won't do simply to blame her and ignore systemic pressures on teachers. As parents, as citizens, the surrounding community also needs to exercise good judgment about what schools are expected and enabled to do.

The remainder of this chapter considers the ethics of collaboration by engaging issues of responsibility and power. It does so mainly through the lens of philosophical texts written in response to notorious instances of the dark side of collaboration, events that occurred when power was exercised tyrannically and violently. While there has been relatively little written by philosophers about collaboration *per se*— readers will note that this book has mainly teased ideas about collaboration out of texts that are more squarely about friendship, loyalty, democracy, and political obligation—a notable exception is Hannah Arendt's post-Second World War writing, especially *Eichmann in Jerusalem*. Near the end of that book, Arendt bears witness to the support many ordinary people across Europe provided to Hitler's regime between 1933 and 1945. While the government-directed genocide and wars of aggression committed by Nazi Germany might seem too removed from contemporary schools to have any relevance to educators, there are sound reasons to turn to philosophical reflections on the Second World War collaborations. For one, it was in response to citizens' support of genocidal political regimes that philosophers significantly rethought the responsibilities that experiences of collective action create. Whether we find ourselves part of a collective by chance, force, or choice, the mere fact of our participation burdens us with responsibilities, though the nature of our involvement shapes the nature of those burdens. The extremes of totalitarianism, which raised existential questions about what it meant simply to go about one's day-to-day business with others, prompted post-war philosophers to shine fresh light on the ways in which everyday instances of working together make us responsible for results of "groupwork" that turn out to be other than we intended.

Philosophical responses to the Second World War collaborations also provide keen insights into the dynamics of power in collective endeavors. Stunned by the apparent willingness of millions of seemingly decent people to provide passive support for murderous mayhem, post-war philosophers returned to the question La Boetie had addressed centuries before. Why do people prop up regimes that strip them of political freedom and the possibility of mutual fellowship? While collaboration at its best rests on an equality of power, with all parties exercising equal agency, collaboration at its worst involves hierarchy, with persons in the middle willing to sell out their fellows for the sake of a relative increase in their own power. In schools, which are simultaneously spaces that foster the collegiality necessary for egalitarian political relationships *and* spaces shaped to serve societies structured by unequal and unjust power relations, both arrangements of power take place—and Arendt's reflections thus apply.

Collective Responsibility

When Arendt wrote about the trial of Adolf Eichmann, the Nazi functionary who organized the roundup and transport to death camps of European Jews, she drew attention to moral and legal questions about how collaborative activities are shaped by power arrangements and produce collective responsibilities, questions that were raised by Nazi war crimes and are continually raised by other state-perpetuated injustices. Arendt's colleague and friend Karl Jaspers also pondered the ascription of guilt for crimes undertaken by state agents obeying orders, as well as whom to punish among the many who had supported, actively or passively, state actions. Later, psychologists like Stanley Milgram undertook studies that explored what cruelty ordinary people were capable of committing when told to do so by authorities. As for the firestorm of controversy lit by *Eichmann in Jerusalem*, it was mainly about the responsibility she attributed to citizens of Germany and other nations, including rabbis who provided Nazi leadership with the names of Jews in their communities. Because the alternative, certainly for the rabbis, could be their own arrest and execution, compliance with Nazi rule was excusable in the eyes of some as self-defense. For Arendt, not so. Those who complied were no Eichmanns. But they were, in at least some sense, working in support of the Nazi regime, along the lines La Boetie had laid out centuries earlier.

In essays she wrote both before and after the *Eichmann* controversy, Arendt explained and justified further her ideas about moral and political responsibility for one's actions in the context of political injustice—which, Arendt recognizes, is the context of *every* real political arrangement, though not all arrangements have been equally unjust or unjust in the same ways. If the wellspring of her interest was the responsibility of ordinary people in totalitarian regimes like Hitler's Reich, what gives her ideas their lasting relevance is their extension to citizens' responsibilities for injustices in other political arrangements, including democracies. Responding to political issues of her day, from the desegregation of Central High School in Little Rock to protests against the Vietnam War, Arendt raised questions that remain essential to any thoughtful approach to the problems of responsibility that collaborative endeavor raises. What is my responsibility for actions undertaken by me as part of a collective? What is my responsibility for actions *not* undertaken by me as part of a collective—my sins of omission, as it were? What difference does my access to power make? Am I (in part or in whole) excused from responsibility if I would have run a serious risk in refusing to collaborate? If I did not know the consequences of the actions the collective was undertaking? If I could have known those consequences but did not try to find out?

"[W]hat disturbed us," wrote Arendt, "was the behavior not of our enemies but of our friends, who had done nothing to bring this situation about. They were not responsible for the Nazis, they were only impressed by the Nazi success and unable to pit their own judgment against the verdict of History, as they read it."[11] In this context, "friends" surely means fellow citizens as well as personal friends, those from whom one would expect some baseline alliance, some norms of interpersonal respect. Replace "Nazis" with your own political collective and its implied wrongs, and "History" with whatever systemic force seems to you most at work in the thinking of fellow citizens who disappoint you—the invisible hand of the market, or human nature, or perhaps still "history"—and that statement captures the dismay many people feel toward the political affiliations, the solidarities and collaborations, of their own times and places. In contemporary democracies reckoning with histories of colonialism, racial injustice, and the uses of violence, even as they are struggling over with what and how much to reckon—with, that is, the very question of what history is shared and what anyone's responsibility for it is—these questions remain relevant. They are essential to our consideration of collaboration, in schools and outside of them, and they are also part of what distinguishes proximate but distinct modes of affiliation like consent, compliance, complicity, and cooptation. When I collaborate with others, what is my responsibility for the results of the project we undertake together? What difference does the power I have to shape the project's means and ends make?

The actions of totalitarian states in the first half of the twentieth century forced a rethinking of the responsibilities citizens incur as members of collective bodies. Previous political theory, from the Enlightenment onwards, had treated citizenship mainly in terms of consent and representation. It considered the legitimacy of government as resting on the consent of the governed, and it explored how that consent, which is given expressly only in exceptional, not ordinary, instances—by immigrants in citizenship proceedings, for instance, but not by babies born into one polity versus another—was to be gauged. The government to which citizens consent is understood to represent them, though what exactly representation entails has also been elusive and debatable. In undertaking large-scale actions (genocides, wars of aggression) that violated the rights of their own citizens and humanity itself, not as incidental to the regular work of governing but as the very mission toward which the government directed the nation's energies, totalitarian regimes forced political philosophers to reconsider. The express starvation of Ukrainian farmers to speed the creation of the proletariat, the genocide of Europe's Jews to clear land for the German Reich—these were projects that required the mass mobilization of ordinary citizens toward ends they had never expressly agreed to, weren't able to vote against, but also, for the most part, went along with.

Adding to the complexity of citizens' responsibility for government actions, technological advances in surveillance had advanced the power of states to punish non-compliance. George Orwell's *1984*, in which the state is able to track even the placement of a hair between a book's pages, was a post-war work of speculative fiction, but Nazi and Stalinist brutality enacted against farmers and poets, professors and priests, mothers and children, demonstrated to citizens how far the state was able to reach in punishing non-compliance.[12] Retreating to one's library like Montaigne and publishing oblique references to counter-authoritarian texts was never an option for everyone, but as mass literacy and the breakdown of old aristocracies made the option more widely available, modern totalitarian regimes closed it off. The range and efficacy of modern bureaucracies also engaged more people in direct contributions to state violence than had previously been possible. People contributed to wars of aggression simply by going to their jobs in offices and factories. It had always been possible to stir mobs into violent action; genocide could now be organized distantly and dispassionately. To what extent were ordinary citizens *responsible* for what was carried out in their names and by means of their ... well, what to call it? Support? Apathy? Compliance? Complicity? Collaboration?

In a series of 1945 lectures, published as *The Question of German Guilt*, Karl Jaspers kicked off post-war conversations about the responsibilities a person incurs simply by being part of a collective. Jaspers teases apart and labels four different kinds of guilt. Critics of his account, starting with Arendt, suggested that "guilt" was the wrong word for some of these and suggested "responsibility" instead. In revising Jaspers's terms and delineations, his critics also rendered his arguments relevant to other instances of collective wrongdoing. Yet for all its limitations, Jaspers's work is a good place to start because it raises important themes that run through the literature that follows. Jaspers introduces the idea of responsibility for actions that were undertaken not by me but in my name, which he calls political guilt and Arendt reconfigures as collective responsibility. He emphasizes the significance of power and agency, which are necessary to any ascription of responsibility, as persons are responsible only to the extent that they had the agency to act otherwise. And Jaspers stresses the importance of judgment.

Jaspers formulates political guilt in contradistinction to criminal guilt, the guilt that comes from having committed a crime. One only ever commits crimes as an individual. Though crimes can certainly be committed by individuals acting together, it is individuals who carry out the actions that constitute the crime, and each individual is guilty for the part he or she played. "Crimes," furthermore, in contrast to other kinds of wrong, "are acts capable of objective proof and violate unequivocal laws," Jaspers says.[13] For there to have been a crime, there needs to have been a law that was contravened. Jaspers wrote this before the Nuremberg trials, but this is the kind of guilt that was applied to the leaders convicted there. (That their convictions required the invention of international criminal law, a new kind of law that falls outside any national legal system, only emphasizes Jaspers's point.) Political guilt, in contrast, "results in my having to bear the consequences of the deeds of the state whose power governs me and under which I live," says Jaspers. Everybody has to bear the consequences because "[e]verybody is co-responsible for the way he is governed."[14] Unlike criminal guilt, political guilt falls on persons as members of the collective regardless of the individual actions they took. It extends to deeds that are not illegal, and even to acts whose harmful effects were not necessarily intended but have caused harm all the same.

As for Jaspers's other two categories, moral guilt is my responsibility for deeds I commit that may not be crimes but are still wrongs. In the situation I find myself in, whether it is a democracy or a totalitarian regime, a time of peace or a time of war, I share responsibilities with my fellow citizens but I remain an individual deciding which of the real choices available to me I shall make, and, like criminal guilt, moral guilt is an individual matter. "Jurisdiction" of moral guilt, says Jaspers, "rests with my conscience, and in communication with my friends and intimates who are lovingly concerned about my soul."[15] Lest this limited jurisdiction let persons off too easily—after all, if *my* conscience doesn't trouble me, and if I only make friends whose concern doesn't extend to those my deeds have harmed, I'd seem to be bound by no morals whatsoever—Jaspers balances it with metaphysical guilt. Of this, he says, "There exists a solidarity among men as human beings that makes each co-responsible for every wrong and every injustice in the world, especially for crimes committed in his presence or with his knowledge. If I fail to do whatever I can do to prevent them, I too am guilty."[16]

Arendt offers "collective responsibility," with the polity serving for her as the relevant collective, as a better term for what Jaspers calls political guilt. The problem with "guilt," as Arendt saw it, was that in saying "all Germans share in the guilt for the Nazi regime," leaders like Eichmann were rendered no guiltier than an ordinary housewife who simply went about her business. "Where all are guilty," she points out, "nobody is."[17] "Guilt, unlike responsibility," she says, "always singles out; it is strictly personal."[18] People who say they *feel* guilty for what others did, Arendt contends, are engaging in a misplaced sentimentality that detracts attention from the actual guilt of actors whose malfeasance is thereby watered down. But this need not and does not let the ordinary housewife off the hook. Although she is not guilty, she is responsible.

As for who is included in the ascription of collective responsibility, Arendt says two conditions have to be present. "I must be held responsible for something I have not done, and the reason for my responsibility must be my membership in a group (a collective) which no voluntary act of mine can dissolve, that is, a collective that is utterly unlike a business partnership which I can dissolve at will."[19] If I did it myself or if I could have left the group once I saw what it was up to—if the group were a mob, say, or a business racket, or a nefarious political party—then my actions were mine as an individual, and we are back in the realm of guilt. Collective responsibility only applies to deeds that were undertaken by a collective I cannot leave. I could, theoretically and sometimes actually, renounce my citizenship and become the citizen of another nation, but to do that is simply to exchange one set of collective responsibilities for another. The fact that the deeds were done in one's name—as a German, say, or as an American—rather than by oneself is what gives collective responsibility its special character.

While Jaspers's account was all about German guilt, Arendt's writing on collective responsibility took up Americans' collective responsibility for race-based injustices and for the Vietnam War, the major issues of the time when she was writing about the topic. Two essays that explicitly address education, "Reflections on Little Rock" and "The Crisis in Education," hold adults responsible, collectively, for problems that Americans, as Arendt saw it, had tried to solve by foisting onto schoolchildren. In "Reflections on Little Rock," Arendt expresses frustration that, in her view, adults declined to address racial discrimination themselves and instead sent Black children into hostile, previously all-white schools, as the foot soldiers of progress.[20] Her challenge was not to racial equality, which she fully supported, but to the eagerness of Americans responsible for the problem—white adults—to ask Black children to solve it. In "The Crisis in Education," she generalizes that point and places responsibility for the world in the hands of adults, not children. Regardless of whether readers agree with Arendt's analysis of school desegregation, or with her assessment of children's participation in politics—many do not—it's worth taking seriously her point that in delegating to the next generation the solution of problems adults cannot or will not address, adults are abdicating their collective responsibility.

Even reconstrued as responsibility instead of guilt, however, this collective burden can seem rather unfair—why should *I* be held responsible for acts I did not commit, just because I had the chance misfortune to be born here and now rather than in some other time and place? For Jaspers and Arendt, fairness is beside the point—persons *just are* born into particular political circumstances. Such is the human condition. Left unanswered by their analyses, though, are questions about just which deeds were done in *my* name. Why should I identify myself by nationality, rather than by some other marker of identity, including some markers that might have set me at an angle to the collective's sense of in whose name it was acting—my gender, say, or my race or ethnicity? Those affiliations are at least as difficult to dissolve as citizenship status. If I happen to be a Black American, in what sense were Jim Crow laws made "in my name," or in that of my Black ancestors? What would be my collective responsibility for such laws? If I am a British citizen whose parents were immigrants from former British colonies, what, across the history of what is now the United Kingdom, was done in my name? Does it matter what role my ancestors played? If we are assessing responsibility in respect to events that took place in the past, in other words, how does the fact play in that I, not having been alive to exercise agency, had no part in that past, and perhaps wouldn't have been considered part of the political collective even if I had been alive at that time? And—most importantly—what relevance does my collective responsibility (or non-responsibility) for what happened in the past have to my collective responsibility for events in the *future*, recognizing that any future is to some extent built upon that past?

Because of such perplexities, Iris Marion Young suggests a somewhat different take. Membership in a political group turns out to be too nebulous a source of responsibility for justice, she thinks, so she proposes instead what she calls "the social connection model." Importantly for us, this model hinges even more than Arendt's on an implicit notion of collaboration. Young is concerned with structural injustices that, as she sees it, cannot be blamed on any particular actor or even institution. To address such injustices, she reconfigures Arendt's ideas about guilt versus responsibility, individual agent versus social structure. She illustrates her ideas using the example of housing insecurity, an injustice that results from a plethora of actions and choices, individual and collective. Young disagrees sharply with theorists who explain social injustices like this one wholly in terms of "personal responsibility," tracing adversities back to misguided individual choices (e.g., to leave secondary school, thus making it difficult to earn a living wage) or to "bad apples" (e.g., sleazy landlords). Yet she also disagrees with theories that explain everything in terms of social structures, fully discounting the role of individuals. Most plausible, she says, is to understand any particular structural injustice, like housing insecurity, in terms of disparate choices made by disparate individuals, not all of which were in any way "wrong" (the business decision to undertake profitable construction projects, for instance, or the chance circumstance of having a baby, or a vote for particular zoning regulations and interest rates that seemed reasonable enough). All of these unconnected actions contribute to social structures. Although each is innocuous in itself, their effects combine to create injustice. The individuals who undertake them, in Young's view, are responsible for these effects inasmuch as their actions played a part in creating and upholding the structures—housing markets, for instance—that they create, regardless of intent. If those structures are unjust, everyone who took part shares in the responsibility for that injustice. This makes responsibility usefully forward-looking, a matter of what I can do in the future.

"Our responsibility," Young says, "derives from *belonging together with others in a system of interdependent processes of cooperation and competition* through which we seek benefits and aim to realize projects."[21] It is the fact of our working together—of our seeking benefits and aiming to realize our projects through political and social collectives—that renders us responsible. Young's model reminds us that in a certain sense we are all collaborators, albeit often unintentionally, in the sense that our actions and choices prop up unjust structures, but her insistence on individual agency is a simultaneous reminder that we are never fully bound to preordained outcomes by the political and social structures we find ourselves in. Only if we pay attention to those structures and our own actions within them, however—to the dynamics of choral competitions, pressures from parents and administrators, economic imperatives, and so forth—and only if we take responsibility for adjusting those dynamics and their outcomes are we able to be collaborators in the best sense and not in the worst.

Power and Agency

Tied up in each of these accounts of the special kind of responsibility to which collective endeavor gives rise are issues of power and agency. Before delving deeper into those, note that throughout the above discussion, different words for collective endeavor, each with its own nuances, have been used. We *cooperate* and we *compete*, we are *complicit* or *compliant*. *Collaboration* in its broadest sense of "working together" can be understood as including all of these as subtypes. At the same time, the specific nuances it picked up in the Second World War, of working hand in glove with an enemy regime, also point to a specific configurations of power and agency in some of its available uses that contrasts with the connotations of other words.

Cooperation (from *co*: together and *operari*: to work) carries the most generic sense of joint endeavor and is also the most uniformly positive. "Cooperator" is never a slur the way "collaborator" can be; to make it an accusation of wrongdoing you'd have to add "with the enemy." Competition (from *com*: together and *petere*: to aim, to seek) implies seeking together but *not* reaching the aim together, in fact quite the opposite. Competition implies striving to achieve by establishing superiority over others who are trying to do the same. Both cooperation and competition, of course, occur in schools. Sometimes people reach their ends together; sometimes the aims are set up as only reachable by some. Which aims are reachable through cooperation and which through competition, as well as the overall proportion of cooperation to competition, says a lot about how a society does, and does not, decide to share its bounty around. Furthermore, the power of those who configure aims as achieved through cooperation or competition has quite a bit to do with how those aims are set up.

Compliance (from *com* = together and *plere* = to fill up, to fulfill) implies fulfilling orders, and also yielding to another's will. It indicates the joint fulfillment of an end but not its joint initiation. It is for the most part expected in hierarchical social and political orders of all sorts, from militaries to religious orders to schools. Collaboration implies a more deliberate commitment to the ends by all parties—not simply following orders, but choosing the ends as also one's own. Hence we talk about an artistic collaboration, or a scientific collaboration, to imply that all parties had an active role in shaping the ends of the project, not just providing the means for carrying it out. As discussed above, complying rather than collaborating does not negate responsibilities, but it does indicate a different, more limited, exercise of agency. Collaboration implies a deliberate, agential choice. As for complicity (from *com* = *together* and *plicat* = *folded*), it falls somewhere in between. Its etymology ties it to the word accomplice; to be complicit is to be folded up in projects with others in a way that indicates more agency than the "just going along" of compliance but less than the "it's a joint project" of collaboration.

Power is an unavoidable aspect of how we work together. "Every human being is fated to be enmeshed in the power relations he lives by," as Jaspers writes. "Failure to collaborate in organizing power relations, in the struggle for power for the sake of serving the right, creates basic political guilt and moral guilt at the same time."[22] Oof, that's a lot to heap onto the presentation of the muscular system! And yet, it has a lot to do with the anxiety school-assigned groupwork creates. Power relations are always being organized in schools, among children, between children and adults, and among adults.

Arendt, thinking specifically about responsibility for organizing political relations under leadership that runs the full range from democratic to dictatorial, suggests four possibilities for action, loosely paraphrased here.[23] First, you can join in enthusiastically, by joining a political party, say, or running for political office. This makes it possible for you to take power and exercise your agency through leadership. Second, you can accept the political relations as they stand and uphold them through your compliance. For the most part, people collaborate in organizing power relations in this second way, which is unproblematic when the political order is generally decent (which does not require that it be perfectly just in all respects). When you pay your taxes, you are collaborating in upholding the power relations you live by. In voting for one political candidate versus another, you are working within, and thereby supporting, the system. Both of these imply consent. When the power relations in which you are enmeshed make demands of you that seem entirely unacceptable, unworthy of your support, there are two other options. You can refuse to take part at all, drop out of the system and live a fully private life, or a public life in a different system. You can take the path of Montaigne writing essays in his library, or draftees who moved to Canada rather than serve in the United States' war in Vietnam. Finally, you can engage in civil disobedience, actively and deliberately defying the system and thereby registering acknowledgement of your responsibility for and to it, even as you refuse to support the particular demands it is making of you. The classic justifications of this approach come from Plato's Socrates and from Henry David Thoreau. As Socrates explains to his friend Crito, in Plato's dialogue by that name, he chooses death over exile when convicted of corrupting the morals of the young by the Athenian court because leaving Athens would prove him to be disrespectful not just of its laws but of law in general, and therefore an unsuitable member of *any* polity. As for Thoreau, he served time in the Concord, Massachusetts jail rather than pay taxes to support a government that legalized human bondage.[24]

Importantly, all of these options involve agency. The argument that no political order can stand without obedience to authority and that individuals thus have no choice but to obey (and thus yield their agency) rests on a fallacy, says Arendt. That fallacy is the equation of obedience with consent. Militaries require obedience, as do church hierarchies, but governments, as James Madison pointed out (and so did La Boétie), rest on the consent of the governed. In politics, claims that someone—Eichmann, for instance—*had no choice but to obey*, or, in other words, that his *agency was necessarily subordinated to the commands of authority*, do pop up, but they do not hold up. "Our use of the word 'obedience' for ... strictly political situations," says Arendt, "goes back to the age-old notion of political science which, since Plato and Aristotle, tells us that every body politic is constituted of rulers and ruled, and that the former give commands and the later obey orders."[25] This age-old notion, she continues, rests on the idea that "every action, accomplished by a plurality of men, can be divided into two stages: the beginning, which is initiated by a 'leader,' and the accomplishment, in which many join to see through what then becomes a common enterprise." This notion, she continues, no longer holds. "In our context, all that matters is the insight that *no man, however strong, can ever accomplish anything without the support of others*."[26] The power to accomplish anything in politics always rests on collaboration among agents—and entails agents being able to choose whether to work together or not.

Here, in order to return to collaboration in schools, we shall have to part ways with Arendt. Having seen the effects of the Nazi party's politicization of children, she argued that political thinking had no place in children's education. Children were, in her view, pre-political—not yet ready to act in the public sphere.[27] The premise of this book, however, is that children *do* engage in political thinking and learning when they collaborate, amongst themselves and under the authority of teachers.[28] Compelling depictions of schoolchildren like *Mindenki* portray (in my view, accurately) the growing understanding of politics that is in fact typical of children. Politics happens among children, and to some extent it mirrors the political world they live, and attend school, within. To be sure, the problems that capture children's attention, their ability to think abstractly about the principles at stake as well as the particulars of the situation, and their ability to organize a collective response are different at age eight than at age eighteen, but the differences are more a matter of growth along a continuum than a sudden shift. Novels like *The Lord of the Flies* that portray children at their collective worst, as well as instances of children engaging in bullying and manipulation, are sometimes held up as proof that children are incapable of decent self-governance, but such arguments are no more persuasive than pointing at Hitler's Germany, ignoring all the rest of modern history, and arguing that adults are categorically incapable of governing themselves. Adults and children alike get it wrong sometimes. They can also get it right.

So let's return to those primary school students who were assigned a collaborative presentation of the muscular system. From the outset, they are enmeshed in power relations, which they might or might not be inclined to uphold. Living in a world structured by gender, racial, social class, and other inequalities, they will begin the project with expectations, perhaps conscious and perhaps not, about who appropriately does what kinds of work, as well as how traits like assertiveness, neatness, scholarly acuity, and amiability are valued in different people. Girls, for instance, are regularly praised for being tidy and agreeable; boys for being bold and original. Black children are often treated as "problems" by white teachers, especially when they are outspoken. Norms are worked into habitual human relations in ways individuals regularly fail to notice. Recent research on microaggressions has uncovered some of the more subtle ways individuals, often unwittingly, reinforce social hierarchies through their interpersonal interactions.[29] Children carry their growing awareness of social norms that reinforce status hierarchies, and the risks of contravening them, into any group project. In Dewey's terms, social norms *continue* into the experience. From the outset, therefore, students participating in groupwork are "enmeshed in the power relations [they live] by." While those power relations may sit comfortably with some individuals, they will not with others. In addition to identity-related power structures, there will also be the unique dynamics of any particular group: who acts as a leader, who is well-organized and committed to getting the task accomplished, who feels disconnected from school. Those idiosyncrasies also come into play. In collaborating on that presentation, the group of students is "organizing power relations," enthusiastically or compliantly or apathetically or resistantly, at the intimate level. The teacher who designed the assignment is likewise enmeshed, and over the course of the school year, as well as previous school years, the students are likely to have picked up at least some of what that means for them.

Since Paul Willis, in *Learning to Labour*, interpreted working class "lads'" resistance to schooling as nascent class consciousness, ethnographic analyses of working-class students and students of color have argued that their frequent refusal to meet school expectations amounts to a refusal to collaborate in their own class and racial subordination. Although their resistance ultimately has the effect of perpetuating class- and race-based inequalities, Willis and others argue that the choice not to comply with schools' demands is an exercise of agency. Willis's "lads" chose working-class solidarity that rewarded them with a sense of pride over throwing in their lot with a disdainful elite. Their stance recognized as a rigged game the invitation schools offer to be complicit in one's oppression by trying and failing. The alternative, success in an unjust system, entails cooptation into the further oppression of the working class—and, sociologists of education extending Willis's work into studies of race add, the cooptation of people of color. Refusal to collaborate with the project of schooling thus amounts to a refusal to become a collaborator in one's own oppression. Whether this kind of resistance is an *effective* means of protest is beside the point. It expresses a political and ethical judgment. From the perspective of the lads, and of wholeheartedly skeptical critics of contemporary schooling more generally, collaboration in the negative sense of throwing in one's lot with illegitimate authorities might be just the word to use for a great deal of schoolwork.

Though differently now than in Willis's account of an older mode of capitalist school-to-factory-floor process, collaboration in the sense of "selling out" may still be what students who adapt themselves to the demands of contemporary schools are invited to engage in. Drawing on a lifetime of research into how workers maintain their self-respect, Richard Sennett argues in *The Culture of the New Capitalism* that traditional workplace bureaucracy, such as that encountered by Willis's lads, is increasingly replaced by what he nicknames the MP3 model. The old model was an immutable hierarchy, in which workers at various levels took orders from above and gave orders down the chain of command. Through faithful service, good fortune, and some measure of talent, workers could hope to advance up the bureaucracy, earning better pay and prestige. Although this "iron cage" was in many ways restrictive, Sennett argues, it provided a narrative structure that made sense of a person's work life, and, paradoxically, it allowed for a measure of freedom.[30] (Here's a different take on La Boetie's puzzle!) Workers in a corporation Sennett studied "certainly felt caged in by the corporation's self-maintaining structures. But within these confines they negotiated the concrete things they were told to do and interpreted the meaning, for them as individuals, of moving from one department to another .... Performing [these small translations] afforded people in the corporation a sense of their own agency."[31] In the "new capitalism" of the past few decades, however, as workplaces have been reorganized for maximum flexibility, corporations have ceased to provide careers, in the sense of lifelong employment. Instead, individuals are expected to move from job to job, picking up new skills, replacing old relationships with new ones, and all at a fairly rapid pace. If the old model was like an album, designed to play songs in one order, the new one is like an MP3 player, which exponentially expands listening options but provides no structure and no narrative.

"Good collaborators," in the sense in which schools typically use the word, are exactly what the MP3 workplace needs. It is hardly surprising, then, that collaboration has become a business buzzword. Nor is it surprising that school systems whose primary aim increasingly is thought to be producing good employees echo this enthusiasm. In school-assigned group work, good collaborators typically take up a task designed by someone else, to meet someone else's ends, and they put forth a decent effort without questioning the fairness of the arrangement or the value of the project. Similarly, the ideal worker in the "new capitalism" realizes that self-interest requires her to align her actions with the interests of those in power, to build and abandon relationships quickly, and not to be tied down by loyalties to colleagues, geographic location, or friends and family. She needs to be able to pick up and move—department, job, home—at the will of her employer, and with each move she will be held fully accountable for her choices and actions. Arguably, children are encouraged to be "good collaborators" because most group work, with its false autonomy and façade of shared interests, is a good preparation for corporate workplaces as Sennett describes them. As thicker political and ethical relationships are replaced with short-term contractual relationships, not just the working class but the professional class as well is asked to collaborate in its own disempowerment.

In an era that aims to replace teaching as a lifetime career with quick certification programs, replace union members with short-term employees who burn out and move on, and replace professional autonomy with accountability mechanisms that blame teachers for failures rooted in complex social circumstances, it is unsurprising that teachers, too, are asked to be good collaborators. With resources limited and the public system threatened by privatization, even parents need to be asked for their collaboration. When students, teachers, and parents are asked to be "good collaborators," the phrase invokes both the autonomous choice and knowledge that the new economy celebrates (though mainly as pseudo-choices and shallow knowledge) and the deficits of loyalty to one's own community that it requires.[32] Totalitarianism, it seems, may not be the only soil in which collaboration's dark side flourishes.

CHAPTER FOUR

Collegiality and Consent

"The Game of Village" is a program in which children build a miniature town and run it themselves. Children everywhere spontaneously make play worlds—in cardboard boxes, with blocks, using natural materials outside—that mix the realities they are coming to understand with other possibilities their imaginations conjure up. Village starts with that impulse and adds a bit of structure, as well as materials and tools that encourage craft learning. To begin, children make "peeps," miniature people with wire skeletons wrapped in yarn and topped with clay or wooden heads. Clothes are sewn, or, more ambitiously, knit. A peep is an individual in its own right, not a representation of the child or any real person. My own peep, Zbyszek, is a Polish man from the foothills of the Tatry mountains with a career in public health and an adopted son named Emile. Children's peeps include a large number of rock stars, equestrians, astronauts (and the occasional space alien), chefs, and race car drivers, as well as pretty much every other kind of character a child might find worth exploring. At Village, the child and the peep function as partners, with the child building a house for the peep to live in and the peep carrying out a life in the town, perhaps starting a bakery or running a stable or performing in a band. Each peep/child partnership gets a plot of land on which to live, which might be a few square feet outside or a share of a sheet of plywood serving as the town's land indoors. Using their plots of land as collateral, they can get loans from the Peep Bank, which they can then use to buy the materials at the Peep Store they need to build their houses.

Because children play, peeps and their communities take on a life of their own. Unlike simulations, in which potential outcomes are determined by algorithm, games of Village have the social, political, and material complexity of real life that play imbues them with. Peeps are quickly instilled with the emotional weight that children's play attaches to otherwise inanimate things, and peep interactions play out the desires and contentions that arise in any human social group. While children of all ages make play worlds, Village is designed for children aged nine to thirteen, developmentally able to hit a nail with a hammer and sew miniature clothing and increasingly able to grasp and ponder abstract ideas. The Village is material as much as it is imagined, with houses made of wood and plexiglass, land that can have streams running on it (inside, with the help of pumps, as well as outside), and peep inhabitants subject to injury and loss. Children open businesses, write books for peeps, and create meticulously landscaped terrain. As things go right and go wrong, the participants need to work together to make collective decisions and solve problems. They need to collaborate.

Some of the decisions villagers face come up in every program. The village needs a name, and that needs to be chosen together. Although each child-peep partnership gets a privately owned piece of land on which to build a house, the rest of the land is owned collectively, and villagers need to decide what to do with it, as well as how to spend the public money that all villages are given at the start. Other decisions are more idiosyncratic. When a boy decided to pen up some of the snails that were on his land, for the purpose of domesticating them he said, another child objected. They were wild animals, she protested, and had the right to roam free. Could snails be captured and held in pens or not? The town discussed the matter and eventually made a law that "you may not capture wild animals, but you may gently move them off your land." For the ten-year-olds, this question was entirely about the treatment of the snails.

For eleven- and twelve-year-olds, it was about the management of wild animals more broadly, rabbits should they wander in for instance, or birds. The thirteen-year-olds started to wonder about the principles of ownership, beyond animals, because the question of whether or not you have a right to animals if they're on your land rests on the question of what grounds anyone has for claiming ownership of land, especially given that it was all taken by force from someone else if you go far enough back in history. Those broader questions had to be left unresolved because the ten-year-olds reminded their peers not to lose track of the snails.

Villages are understood as existing within the Republic of Peeps, represented by the adults running the program, who have the authority to enforce a scant handful of national laws (no hurting people or peeps, tools must be used properly, and everyone has to clean up at the end of the day), and who otherwise count as ordinary citizens of the village. There are also rules of the game: everyone makes a peep, peeps are owed child-made dwellings, for the most part everything in the Village has to be made or found at Village, and the village starts off as a democracy, with all children and peeps sharing in collective decision-making. The rules all flow from the shared objectives: to build a miniature village together and to have a good time doing it. The rest is up to the children and their peeps. These rules of the game make Village significantly different from school, or most workplaces. The power relations in which children are enmeshed at Village are relatively egalitarian, with adults having power to do things like provide or deny access to power drills but not to determine what counts as success. Building a miniature village leaves room for a wide variety of individual aspirations and accomplishments, whereas schools (to be fair, for some very legitimate reasons) expect everyone to learn more or less the same things. At Village, children can spend all their time working on what interests them, and the diversity of their achievements is generally to the collective advantage. A child who sews and decorates a yurt for her peep contributes as much as the child who knocks together a plywood house and spends the rest of his time making a ski jumping course with a track for peep-scaled skis that roll.

In 1994, I moved to Krakow, Poland, to teach English but mostly to run Village as an after-school program. For several summers before that, I had been the co-director of a five-week Village day camp in New Hampshire. In New Hampshire, children proposed and agreed every summer that there should be a government, that government's most important feature was its inclusion of everyone, and that therefore all decisions should be made in a town meeting format. Without fail, they raised these ideas at the start of the village's creation, and for the most part they stuck to them. Direct democracy of this sort was familiar to them, as the small towns around worked this way and had for a long time. Like many adults, they quickly discovered that working together to solve public problems by means of open discussions was time-consuming and, for many of them, dull, so a king or an oligarchy would occasionally be proposed for the sake of efficiency. If a proponent succeeded in making autocracy sound like a terrific lark and a painless path to gaining back an hour of time each day, those proposals passed. Within a week, the king or the oligarchs had usually made some unpopular (though not always unreasonable) decision, and the town's citizens would revert to direct democracy.

I wondered what would happen if children someplace else, without New Hampshire's town meeting tradition, had the chance to play Village. In 1994, Poland seemed the perfect place to find out because adults were also taking charge of their governments, also reimagining political possibilities, and also exploring the promise and frustrations of democratic self-governance. Krakow's Primary School 116 invited me to teach English to children in grades 1–8 and run Village as an extracurricular activity. For a year and a half, Polish children built towns in 1:25 scale, on sheets of plywood rather than an acre of land, pushing aside desks to use a regular classroom as a space for sawing, sewing, hammering, baking miniature pizzas in a toaster oven, and legislating. Or not. Polish schoolchildren, it turned out, were far less keen than New Hampshire children to set up a government. When it was suggested to them as a means of solving collective problems, they looked puzzled. *You* make the rules, they'd say. That's *your* job. We don't want to. We want to build our houses.

The children did, however, work together in other ways that were unlike anything I'd seen in New Hampshire. When Anna came back to school after a week's absence, one of the boys hollered to the group that someone needed to help her because she'd fallen behind in house-building. It was informally agreed that Piotrek, as the most skillful carpenter, should do that, and as soon as it was decided that he was the person to help, he put aside his own projects until she'd caught up. This kind of informally organized mutual aid was repeated as problems arose, even as the children resisted the idea of solving problems by means of government. They were good *koledzy* to one another, as I frequently heard their teachers remind them to be. Where New Hampshire children solved the problems of coordinating their collective labor by means of formal (or formal-ish, at least) self-governance, these children in Krakow solved those problems through informal practices of collegiality. New Hampshire children helped each other out, to be sure, but I never heard them do it in that quasi-public way. A friend would help a friend. In Krakow, the expectation was hollered to the whole group, everyone was responsible relative to their means, and everyone counted as *koledzy*.

Both collegiality and consent to democratic government, that is, proved to be decent means of solving problems raised in the course of creating a village. Tracing those two words back to their roots, as the previous chapter did with *co*-words like collaboration and complicity, turns up a surprising overlap. Like other *co*— words, both have Latin origins, with colleague (and its Polish cognate *kolega,* of which *koledzy* is the plural) indicating someone with a shared capacity to make decisions. The word came into English by way of French, where it meant more specifically a *work* partner, an office mate. In English, the word has maintained that specificity; to call someone a colleague is to imply someone with whom one works. In Polish it means an acquaintance more broadly, applied to anyone with whom one has a friendly relationship on the basis of things done together, now or in the past. It wouldn't be much of a stretch to say that the Polish use of *koledzy* implies that the social world is a shared space of occupations, a world in which people work together and—crucially—share the authority for making decisions about that work. The word colleague is related to delegate, and like a delegate, a colleague is empowered to act on the workplace's behalf. But the prefix *de*— indicates down, so a delegate is someone to whom power devolves, whereas a colleague is an equal partner. This places some limits on who counts as a *kolega*. In schools, your classmates are your *koledzy*; your teacher is not. So the idea at the root of collegiality goes beyond warm feelings and friendliness to include a recognition of the other as one's equal in authority. Colleague captures the equality of agency that is part of collaboration in its narrower sense, but unlike collaborator, colleague also carries the sense of mutual goodwill, of specifically friendly togetherness, especially in its offspring *collegiality*. One may not always feel collegial toward all of one's colleagues, but the word invokes that hope.

As for consent, the idea can be traced back to early modern writers—it's implicit in La Boétie's *Voluntary Servitude,* in that idea that only the agreement of the many props up the leader, and that because men are born free and equal their support can be withdrawn—but it got its most famous expression in the United States' *Declaration of Independence*. In that document, five truths are held to be self-evident, and one of these is that "to secure those rights [to life, liberty and the pursuit of happiness], Governments are instituted among Men, deriving their just powers from the consent of the governed."[1] To consent is to agree to the government's exercise of (just) powers. In this, the word's meaning crosses with that root sense of "colleague" as a person whose actions on behalf of a shared objective are recognized as legitimate. If politics is indeed a kind of work, those who consent to the same government are all, also, our colleagues. As for the fellow-feeling aspect of colleague/collegiality, which at first glance consent seems to lack, being a social studies textbook and legalistic sort of word, consider consent's etymology. To consent is, at root, to *feel* together, as the word is derived from Latin *sentire*, the same root that gave us *sentiment*. Etymology doesn't say everything important about a word's meaning, of course, but, in the ways they play out, both collegiality and consent rest on two features: an equality of authority and the friendly feeling that Aristotle called civic friendship. Whether it comes out as the Krakow children's informal practice of mutual aid or as the New Hampshire children's direct democracy, solving the problems that arise through working together demands fellow-feeling *and* shared authority.

There are advantages and disadvantages to both the Krakow children's more informal practices of mutual aid and the New Hampshire children's legislative inclinations, which came out as difficult cases arose. When two boys in a Krakow village both wanted to make and sell furniture, and each claimed to have been the originator of a particular method of chair-construction, they discovered the need to make some laws (and how difficult patent laws are to write). When one New Hampshire village overthrew their short-term king, considerable mollification and restoration of relationships was required to make up for having so quickly lifted and crashed a monarchical career. But this is really to say that whether problems were solved by means of collegiality or consent to government, under neither approach was it possible to neglect the counter-valence of the idea—the joint authority implicit in collegiality or the fellow feeling in consent.

Avoiding Trivialization

At the outset of this book, collaboration was proposed as a replacement word for fraternity, that third and often problematic pillar of democracy. As explained in the Introduction, I also chose it over solidarity because solidarity, a uniformly positive word, conveys none of the undertow that is part and parcel of ties of affection and loyalty. The moral hazards pop up when fraternity and solidarity run into conflicts with equality, and thus the previous two chapters have had quite a bit to say about that democratic ideal. Friendship is an egalitarian relationship, of course. Any actual friendship, to slightly rephrase Jaspers, is fated to be enmeshed in the power relations the friends live by. So the premise of equality as a foundational principle of government also matters, as La Boétie and Forster especially (and poignantly, given their circumstances) recognized, if friendships are to be created and upheld through thick and thin in any social world. The counterpoint, that good politics relies on something like friendship among citizens was pointed out by Aristotle, in his line about why lawgivers value it even more than justice. When power becomes hierarchical, especially when it reaches the extreme at which state violence becomes a constant threat, as for instance under the Nazi regime, persons are incentivized to collaborate not with their fellow citizens but with the regime. Collaboration at its worst works hand in glove with oppression; collaboration at its best dovetails with equality.

What about freedom, that other pillar of liberal democracy? How does it square with collaboration? John Dewey connects the two via a discussion of social control. "I take it," he writes. "that the ordinary good citizen is as a matter of fact subject to a great deal of social control and that a considerable part of this control is not felt to involve restriction of personal freedom."[2] Children's games are Dewey's choice of an illustration. Games, importantly, have rules. In some games, like tag or ghost-in-the-graveyard, the rules are uncodified, though children are keenly aware of the rules that govern play, whereas in others, like football and basketball, the rules are standardized by adults. In either case, rules are part of the game, not outside of it. "No rules, then no game; different rules, then a different game. As long as the game goes on with a reasonable smoothness, the players do not feel that they are submitting to external imposition but that they are playing the game."[3] Rules of a game, that is, function to keep the game going, rather than as impositions of personal power. When a call is made that an individual player objects to, the objection is that the rule wasn't upheld fairly, not that there shouldn't be rules. To be sure, sometimes the rules themselves are renegotiated, as for instance when children want to play but have too few players, or are playing basketball in a driveway instead of a court, but in such instances, the quality of the game remains the objective. If personal interest *is* perceived to be some player's motivation, that person is likely to be dismissed as too bossy. The point of renegotiating rules, as well as upholding them fairly, is to keep playing. For Dewey, this feature of games goes to show that "control of individual actions is effected by the whole situation in which individuals are involved, in which they share and of which they are co-operative or interacting parts."[4] What is true of competitive games, Dewey thinks, is all the more true of activities that are inherently cooperative. Activities that are genuinely *social,* Dewey suggests, keep themselves going without anyone feeling their freedom impinged upon.

Fraternity, liberty, and equality, "take on a veridical and directive meaning only when they are construed as marks and traits of an association which realizes the defining characteristics of a community," argues Dewey, and I agree.[5] Otherwise, they are "hopeless abstractions. Their separate assertion leads to mushy sentimentalism or else to extravagant and fanatical violence which in the end defeats its own aims."[6] What I have tried to argue over the course of this book is that a great deal of school, and business-world, talk of "collaboration" falls into exactly such a trap of mushy sentimentalism. When projects are assigned to students or to educators by higher-ups who control the objectives of the project, who control much of how it is to be carried out, and who control what counts as success, to call it a "collaboration" is to put a veneer of mutuality and empowerment over what is, in fact, merely carrying out a delegated task. And although a group project to create a presentation of the muscular system is a long way from collaborating with the Nazis, it is precisely through the expectation of unthinking compliance, as well as acceptance of the banal with no eye to what it masks, that children (and adults) learn to follow instructions unquestioningly and at worst to be complicit in their own and others' subjugation. Twenty-first-century global capitalism is not Hitler, but it also wreaks extravagant harm on the planet and on the billions who suffer what can reasonably called the violence of its excesses, especially on those rendered most vulnerable by historical legacies of oppression. All the same, I have confidence that, with the use of good judgment, educators can foster the agency and collegiality that enables children to rethink the political forces in which they are enmeshed, rather than passively uphold them.

I have offered children playing The Game of Village as an example of collaboration at its best. It is also impossibly impractical to scale it up and make it available everywhere, and to do so would raise other problems (such as: what if the child who makes yurts never learns to read?). Montessori and Waldorf schools have many of the same qualities (and do teach children to read), but they rely on low teacher – student ratios (which are expensive to provide) and, some have suggested, depend for their success on educated families providing academic foundations that are not universally available to children.[7] From Village's best features, however, it's possible to glean insights into features that good collaborations in real classrooms need to have. A jointly undertaken project, Village is in accordance with children's interests and inclinations. Authority over what transpires lies mostly in the rules of the game; agency, therefore, is in children's hands to an exceptional degree. This does not mean that all collaborations need to be games. Games, rather, illustrate aspects of joint endeavor that are genuinely social. They are just one example of cooperative activity, in which, as Dewey puts it, "it is not the will or desire of any one person which establishes order but the will of the whole group."[8] Classrooms can be genuinely social without being games; the question then becomes what it takes to make them *social*. Social classrooms take up activities whose aims are understood, appreciated, and deemed worthwhile by all who are asked to take up the work. The benefits of accomplishing the project have to accrue, and be understood to accrue, to all. This, of course, is a lot easier to pull off as a summer camp, or an after school activity, in which no one is required to attend, in which there are no state mandates, few parental expectations except that children have fun and come home with all their fingers, and an abundance of nifty tools and materials. Most of what children are required to learn in schools, though, from literacy to math to art to gym, does have a great deal to offer children beyond scores on a standardized test and the promise of future employability. The challenge is to center why *children* should find that education valuable. Not just their parents, or the Department of Education, or future employers, but children themselves.

The above is more easily said than done. Happily, schools offer—or could offer, if they were provided the resources—myriad cooperative activities that are excellent grounds for fostering meaningful collaborations. Bands and choruses and orchestras are one excellent example, as are sports teams. Theater productions. School newspapers, and yearbooks, and literary magazines. It is one of the sorriest effects of declining financial support for public schools, of the focus of schools' limited resources on what can be quantified, and of the intensification of competitive child-raising in recent decades that these activities are less available in schools and less open to all than they should be, and are increasingly framed as opportunities to make your college application stand out. That's in the United States, the context I'm most familiar with; other national systems treat extra-curriculars as less essential aspects of school (if they exist at all). If we took collaboration seriously, perhaps activities like these should be essential aspects of any school—if there were, magically, some way to incorporate them into schooling without then putting adults more fully in charge. Once outsiders start quantifying their accomplishments, they undo all they currently offer as spaces in which children can exercise agency and discover their mutual responsibilities as they work together. That's a big if, given the way schools tend to be run. Shy of that ideal, in schools as we have them now, teachers might still attend to how classroom projects can be made more genuinely social, and therefore meaningfully collaborative. I'd also like to see us all stop calling "collaborations" activities that really aren't. Or that are, more ominously, collaborations in the worst sense of asking for students' complicity with harmful aspects of a social order. As *Mindenki*, and children's literature, and students who love programs like Village but groan at the prospect of groupwork all remind us, from an early age children are savvy as to how much agency they are really being allowed to exercise, what micro-political realities constrain them, and from whom they can expect loyalty. They know what kinds of collaboration are really being asked for. Let's ask for the good kind.

Why Collaboration Matters

As I was finishing this book, two news stories illustrated why it matters how we think about the work we do together—as well as of how immediately people jump to connect schooling and collaboration. In September 2022, the Ukrainian army retook swathes of the northeast that had been under Russian occupation for half a year. In the wake of that victory, the New York Times titled an article about Ukrainian officials' and local townspeople's reckoning with one another's choices, "As Russia Retreats, a Question Lingers: Who Counts as a Collaborator?"[9] The thorniest problems, in the newspaper's account, were posed by the decisions made by teachers. Providers of essential public services were not deemed collaborators when the work they did, like putting out fires and tending the sick, was understood as needing to go on. But schooling? Whether it needed to go on was a question everyone faced during the pandemic, but here with a brutal political twist.[10] Russia's rationale for launching the war was that Ukraine had never been an independent nation and was always part of Russia. This is the narrative Russian-run schools would promote. This dynamic is hardly unique to Russia, as state schools have always provided dominant political groups with a means of reinforcing their political narratives, in liberal democracies as much as in totalitarian systems. The relevant difference is that liberal democracies allow for challenges to those narratives, and, if a majority of citizens can be persuaded, changes. In the United States, schools' narratives were contested in the 1840s by Irish immigrants challenging a curriculum that taught their children to read using the King James Bible, after the Civil War by teachers in formerly Confederate states who taught that war as the "War of Northern Aggression," and by contemporary Black critics who challenge the national narrative of perpetual progress toward equality. Every pluralistic society with a school system has its own version of these conflicts. To school children using any national narrative (and all curricula have a narrative) is to teach them to whom they owe their loyalties, with whom to cooperate, toward what ends to strive. To collaboration's three key questions—With whom? Under what, or whose, authority? Toward what ends?—schools give answers that uphold the dominant political arrangements.

Teachers in Russian-occupied Ukraine were thus suddenly under orders to teach Russia's account. If they didn't quit their jobs, they had to learn over the summer how to teach the Russian curriculum and then, when schools reopened on September 1, put that curriculum into practice. As reported by the New York Times, some teachers reasoned that the difference between a Russian and Ukrainian elementary-grade curriculum was minimal, and that children needed the stability provided by open schools and familiar teachers. Others refused to have anything to do with the Russian school system, giving up their jobs and salaries and subsisting on homegrown vegetables rather than collaborate. Others kept on teaching simply because they needed the money. In response, Ukraine's education ombudsman, Serhiy Horbachov, declared that teachers who agreed to teach the Russian curriculum should lose their credentials. "These people," he said, "absolutely cannot be allowed to work with Ukrainian children."[11]

Ukrainians, and outsiders, can reasonably draw different lines as to what kinds of compliance count as collaboration, but the point is that when people feel themselves under the thumb of oppressors, it *matters* who, and how, their fellows decide to work together. It especially matters in schools. Schools, after all, are where the next generation is figuring out its answers to those questions.

The second story comes from New Hampshire, where annual town meetings include a vote on the school budget. Like many small towns, Croydon NH, population approximately 800, has its own primary school but pays tuition for children past fourth grade to attend public or private schools in neighboring districts, expenses covered by the school budget. Important background to the conflict that erupted is that New Hampshire, a small state with a longstanding libertarian streak—the state's motto is "Live Free or Die"—has recently been the focus of the "Free State Project," which declares itself "a mass migration of more than 20,000 people who have pledged to move to New Hampshire for liberty." Free staters, according to the organization's website, "are busy" doing things like "choosing peaceful resistance to shine the light on the force that is the state," "working to expand individual rights and free markets," and "serving as proponents of liberty in local government."[12] Would-be activists are directed to the project's page promising "an enthusiastic legion of liberty-minded activists ready to help." (Responsibility is radical and personal, apparently, but still best achieved by a like-minded group.) At Croydon's March 2022 town meeting, one such liberty-minded activist proposed cutting the school budget by more than half. His wife, who was the head of the school board that had proposed the original budget and also a free stater, agreed. When it came to a vote, the reduced budget passed, 20–14.[13] At that level of funding, the town would no longer be able to pay for Croydon's students to attend regional public schools. The town's K-4 school would have to fire more than half its staff, leaving its children to be taught through a private contractor by uncertified "guides." Voters who had not shown up to the town meeting, trusting that others were taking care of the decisions that needed to be made, were stunned—and angry.

They had one recourse. Under New Hampshire law, a town can hold a revote if more than 50 percent of all the voters on the town's checklist show up at a meeting to reconsider. Residents filed a petition to hold a revote, and in May, another meeting was held. Because the validity of the revote rested on the presence of a quorum (in this case 283 of the 565 voters on the town's checklist), proponents of the cut were encouraged to stay home. Supporters of the original budget, calling themselves "We Stand Up for Croydon Students," figured out the state's laws and then knocked on doors, held phone banks, and posted yard signs.[14] At a May meeting, voters approved restoration of the original budget in a landslide, 377–2. It was a victory—and, Croydon voters told reporters, a lesson in the importance of taking their democratic responsibilities seriously.

It matters *how* we work together, but if the story of Croydon's school budget has a moral, it's that it matters *that* we work together. A new school budget will come up at next year's town meeting, and voters will need to show up, year after year. Collaboration is togetherness; it's also labor. The labor is what makes the togetherness real. That school system that kept its funding—let's hope the children it educates understand that too.

NOTES

Chapter 1

1   Deak, *Minkenki* (Sing).
2   Dewey, *The School and Society*, 7.
3   Dewey, *Democracy and Education*, 81–2.
4   Dewey, *Democracy and Education*, 82.
5   Dewey, *Democracy and Education*, 82.
6   Rawls, *A Theory of Justice*.
7   Dewey, *Democracy and Education*, 83.
8   Dewey, *Democracy and Education*, 83.
9   Dewey, *Democracy and Education*, 87.
10 Dewey, *Democracy and Education*, 85.
11 Dewey, *The Public and Its Problems*, 176.
12 Dewey, *The Public and Its Problems*, 175.
13 Dewey, *School and Society*, 14; *Democracy and Education*, 87; *Public and Its Problems*, 176.
14 I first addressed these experiences and ideas in "Collaboration: The Politics of Working Together."
15 Political philosopher Danielle Allen has written eloquently about the difference between "oneness" and "wholeness," praising the latter idea for the room it leaves for pluralism. See Allen, Danielle. *Talking to Strangers* and *Our Declaration*. Biographers agree that Franklin probably spoke these words attributed to him or something close, though there is no conclusive record.
16 Aristotle, *Nicomachean Ethics*. The passage is in book 8, 1155a. In *Talking to Strangers*. Danielle Allen connects Aristotle's ideas about friendship and justice to contemporary race relations and citizenship in the United States, arguing that democracy's success depends upon friend-like relations among citizens.

Chapter 2

1 In her 2008 Harvard commencement speech, Rowling discusses working in the African research department at Amnesty International, which she says "informed much of what she wrote" in the Harry Potter novels. There, she regularly read, overheard, and saw evidence of the suffering of ex-political prisoners who had chosen to risk everything for their political convictions. Rowling, "The Fringe Benefits of Failure and the Importance of Imagination."

2 Judith Shklar says that "fidelity" is the name for what we owe friends, "loyalty" for what we owe states, and "commitment" what we owe values. This distinction can be helpful in thinking about the differences between what we owe individuals, collectivities, and ideals. Philosophers who have written about these allegiances have not always used those words as Shklar defines them, however, nor, therefore, have I.

3 Rowling, *Harry Potter and the Sorcerer's Stone*.

4 Montaigne, *Complete Works*, 169. The historical accuracy of Montaigne's account of his friendship with Boétie, and his reasons for presenting Boétie as he did, are usefully discussed by Montaigne's biographer Philippe Desan in *Montaigne: A Life*.

5 Montaigne, *Complete Works*, 171.

6 Most translations of Aristotle's *Nicomachean Ethics* call these "virtue" friendships, but philosopher John Cooper suggests "character" as a better word. On examination of Aristotle's examples of this most "perfect" kind of friendship, Cooper concludes that "on Aristotle's theory what makes a friendship a virtue-friendship is the binding force within it of *some* – perhaps, for all that, partial and incomplete – excellence of the character, and the perfect friendship of the perfectly virtuous is only an especially significant special case of this. For this reason, it seems preferable to refer to friendship of the central kind not, as Aristotle most often tends to do, as 'friendship of the good' but, as he sometimes calls it, "friendship of character .... The expression 'character friendship' brings out accurately that the basis for the relationship is the recognition of good qualities of character, without in any way implying that the parties are moral heroes." John Cooper, "Aristotle on the Forms of Friendship," 319–20.

7   Aristotle, *Nicomachean Ethics.*
8   Montaigne, *Complete Works,* 169.
9   Ibid., 164.
10   Ibid., 164.
11   Ibid., 164.
12   Ibid., 175.
13   Francois Rigolot suggests another interpretation in his essay "Friendship and Voluntary Servitude: Plato, Ficino and Montaigne." Rigolot notes that the phrase "voluntary servitude" appears twice in the two translations of Plato's *Symposium* Montaigne is most likely to have read—Ficino's Latin, where it appears as *voluntaria servitus* and Le Roy's French translation, as *la servitude voluntaire* (La Boétie's title). In Plato's *Symposium,* Pausanias uses the phrase in a speech about friendship, a speech that also mentions two famous Athenian friends, Harmodius and Aristogiton, who overthrew the tyranny of Pisistratus. These friends are also named by La Boétie in one of the passages of *Voluntary Servitude* that contrast man's natural inclinations to friendship with the obsequiousness required by tyrants. In this intertextual connection of both La Boétie's discourse and Montaigne's *Of Friendship* to Plato's *Symposium,* Rigolot reads the paradoxical presence and absence of the discourse in the *Essays* as a clue that points to a second set of meanings a reader could attach to voluntary servitude—and to *Voluntary Servitude.* A deeper foray into Plato's understanding of friendship and political obligation, as, arguably, picked up by Montaigne, would take us into an intellectually rewarding exploration of Renaissance humanism as it understood itself but very far from this book's aims. For the curious reader, Plato's *Symposium,* as well as *Lysis,* has much to say about friendship and the good life.
14   Montaigne, *Complete Works,* 169.
15   Desan, *Montaigne.*
16   Desan, 117.
17   La Boétie, author's translation. I have listed in the references both the Hackett translation and the text in French available online. The Hackett translation, while a good rendition overall, makes a few word choices, especially in translating "égaux"—equals—in one place as "comrades" and another as

"free"—that blur what La Boétie is saying about friendship. The French trinity of *liberté, égalité* and *fraternité* are interconnected but not interchangeable. Other English translations of *Voluntary Servitude* have also made word choices that slant the text's political implications, picking up some connections and nuances at the expense of others. Before the 2012 translation, the available English version was a 1944 translation by Harry Kurtz that was very much influenced by the anti-Nazi politics of his moment. The Online Library of Liberty has a version that makes La Boétie sound like an economist arguing against taxes. Politicized interpretations were, of course, the text's fate in its time as well, as Montaigne lamented.

18 On this, and the conception of *fraternité* that motivated revolutionaries, see Carole Pateman, *The Sexual Contract*.
19 La Boétie, author's translation.
20 Ibid.
21 Ibid.
22 Ibid.
23 Desan, pp. 121–3.
24 Montaigne, *Complete Works,* 165.
25 Rowling, *Harry Potter*, 272–3.
26 Ibid., 306.
27 For Plato, Aristotle and Cicero, the convictions of the truly virtuous would also be, in important senses, true. This principle also, neatly, prevents genuine ethical conflict between the personal and political loyalties of good men. Montaigne, as he explains in his essay *Of Cannibals*, takes a more relativist approach, reasoning that each person upholds the virtues of his own social world.
28 Royce, *The Philosophy of Loyalty,* 15.
29 Royce, *The Philosophy of Loyalty,* 16–17 emphasis in original. In keeping with the conventions of his time, Royce uses "man" for the universal person, but he does include women among his examples of the loyal, e.g. "lovers" (given the era, readers would presumably have read this as referring to heterosexual women and men) and mothers. On pp. 183–5, he uses the extended example of an educated woman torn between the demands of career and family to illustrate conscience—concluding that it matters not which cause she chooses, only *that* she choose a

cause and be loyal to it. Indeed, when he returns to her choice, on page 193, he says that "the life of the devoted sister or aunt" and "the life of the successful servant of a profession" are each "a whole life." "No mortal knows which is the better for your world," and therefore there is no correct choice. Given that conventional morality is still hung up on whether or not women's virtue can include commitment to a career, Royce's use of this example seems a genuine indication that his conception of moral persons includes women.

30 Ibid., 18–19.

31 Ibid., 19.

32 Ibid., 66.

33 Ibid., 94, emphasis added.

34 In 1908, the same year he published *The Philosophy of Loyalty*, Royce published another book, *Race Questions, Provincialism, and Other American Problems*. Contemporary scholars have mixed views of Royce's philosophical work on race; while Royce is more outspokenly critical of racism than nearly all white philosophers of his era, racist ideas also slip into his writing. Whatever readers conclude about how to read texts like this, no one can deny that Royce was thinking hard about the problems posed by racism, provincialism, and the like. In 1914 and 1916, after his career was cut short by a stroke and just before his death in 1916, Royce published two books that addressed the world war, *War and Insurance* and *The Hope of the Great Community*, which make the case for something like the League of Nations. Again, whatever one concludes about the merits of his ideas, he was certainly aware of the hazards of provincial loyalties—and of human beings' psychological need for loyalty, which tends toward ill if not toward good.

35 Royce claims that loyalty is a capacity all human beings share. In Royce's framework, that is, the capacity for loyalty replaces Kantian reason as what makes us the appropriate objects of moral concern, ends in ourselves. Writing in an age when women, Black Americans, and immigrants were frequently excluded from full human personhood by their supposed deficiencies of reason, Royce can be interpreted as suggesting an alternative, and more inclusive, hallmark. On what Royce has to offer feminist scholarship, see Kara Barnette, "Communities, Traitors, and the Feminist Cause."

36 Forster, "What I Believe," 67.
37 Ibid., 67.
38 Ibid., 67. Readers of Forster's *Howards End* (or viewers of
    the 1992 film) will recognize the echo of that book's epigraph:
    "Only Connect." Three momentous decades later, connection
    remains key but the epitaph no longer sufficient.
39 Ibid., 68.
40 Ibid., 68.
41 Ibid., 68.
42 Ibid., 68, emphasis added.
43 Ibid., 69. For readers wondering why "Beloved Republic" is
    capitalized, the phrase appears in *Hertha*, a quasi-mystical
    poem by nineteenth-century poet Algernon Charles Swinburne,
    whose work was widely read in Forster's time but rarely in
    ours. The full line is "Even love, the beloved Republic, that
    feeds upon freedom and lives." Democracy, Forster implies, is
    not and should not be confused with love.

Chapter 3

1   These ideas run throughout Dewey's writing on education but
    are explained most clearly and concisely in *Experience and
    Education*, especially in Chapter 3, "Criteria of Experience."
2   Dewey would use the word "habits." For a fuller explanation of
    what he means by habit, see *Human Nature and Conduct*.
3   Dewey, *Experience and Education,* 37.
4   Ibid., 33.
5   Ibid., 25.
6   Ibid., 27.
7   Joseph Dunne and Shirley Pendlebury, "Practical Reason,"
    195–6.
8   For a rich account of practices, see Alasdair MacIntyre, *After
    Virtue.* 1981.
9   An insightful take on this is suggested by Richard Smith, in
    "Paths of Judgment: the revival of practical wisdom." Martha
    Nussbaum explores the matter of discernment and the roots
    of the idea of practical reasoning in ancient philosophy in *The
    Fragility of Goodness*.

10   See Barbara Stengel, *Responsibility*, for a different but
     congruent account of this word's meaning in educational
     philosophy and practice.

11   Hannah Arendt, "Personal Responsibility under Dictatorship."

12   Stalin's Soviet Union and its eastern empire lends itself to the
     same reflections as Hitler's Germany. That the literature on
     collective responsibility was inspired more by the latter than the
     former has much to do with circumstances during and after the
     war. Intellectuals like Arendt fled west, and Germany, having
     lost the war, was open to scrutiny by the victors and the next
     generation of its own citizens. Only after 1989, when the crimes
     of the 1930s and 1940s were long past, were archives in the
     post-Soviet East opened. A flood of publications on Russian,
     Ukrainian, Belorussian, Polish, and others' responsibility for
     brutalities in what Timothy Snyder calls, in his book of that
     title, "the bloodlands" followed. Among the most powerful
     accounts was Jan Gross's *Neighbors*, which told the story of
     how the Polish citizens of Jedwabne, Poland turned on their
     Jewish neighbors in 1941, murdering in one day hundreds of
     people with whom they had lived peacefully as neighbors. And
     one need not stop there: events in the bloodlands are echoed
     in brutal episodes from the histories of China, Cambodia,
     South Africa, Rwanda, the Jim Crow South, and more.
     There are differences, to be sure, between mob violence and
     bureaucratically managed genocide, but the point is that the
     Nazis had no monopoly on state-supported murder. Nor was the
     Holocaust the only evil unresisted by the majority of citizens.
     That philosophical literature on collective responsibility began
     in response to Nazi Germany has more to do with who was
     publishing philosophy than with any unique national qualities
     of wrongdoing reliant on the coordination of masses of people.

13   Jaspers, *The Question of German Guilt*, 25.

14   Ibid., 25.

15   Ibid., 26.

16   Ibid., 26.

17   Arendt, "Collective Responsibility," 147.

18   Ibid., 147.

19   Ibid., 149.

20   Arendt's interpretation of school desegregation was challenged
     when she wrote it, and it continues to be challenged, on the

grounds that she did not understand the ethical and political commitments of Black Americans that motivated Black parents and children alike. See Kathryn Gines, *Hannah Arendt and the Negro Question*. For additional analysis of her views on education see Chris Higgins, "Education, Crisis, and the Human Condition: Arendt after 50 Years"; Mordechai Gordon, ed., *Hannah Arendt and Education: Renewing Our Common World*; Aaron Schutz, and Marie Sandy, "Friendship and the Public Stage."

21 Young, *Responsibility for Justice*, 105. Emphasis added.

22 Jaspers, *The Question of German Guilt*, 28.

23 Arendt, "Political Responsibility under Dictatorship."

24 On civil disobedience, see Plato, *Crito*, and Henry David Thoreau "Civil Disobedience." Martin Luther King's "Letter from Birmingham Jail" is part of this conversation though a bit different, as King acted in defiance of a government that failed to accord him the full rights of citizenship. Arendt's essay "Civil Disobedience," is one of many takes on the concept. Judith Shklar's *Political Obligation* traces the history of the idea of personal conscience as at odds with political obligation.

25 Arendt, "Political Responsibility under Dictatorship," 46.

26 Ibid., 47. Emphasis added.

27 For discussion of this point, see Schutz and Sandy, "Friendship and the Public Stage"; Schutz "Is Political Education an Oxymoron?"; Levinson, "But Some People Will Not."

28 Criticisms of "Reflections on Little Rock," including those cited in note 20, point out that Arendt had little understanding of the shared African American idea of struggle, which was familiar to Black children as well as adults, suggesting that she significantly misinterpreted children's inevitable awareness of political life from an early age.

29 See Rini, *The Ethics of Microaggression*.

30 Sennett draws this language and analysis from Max Weber, *The Protestant Ethic and the Spirit of Capitalism*.

31 Sennett, *Culture of the New Capitalism*, 35.

32 This analysis of demands on students and teachers, as well as student resistance and the changing career structure of teachers is drawn directly from my article, "Collaboration: The Politics of Working Together."

Chapter 4

1   *The Declaration of Independence*, accessed in Danielle Allen, *Our Declaration*. Allen's account of that document gives depth and richness to words that too easily lose their power through mindless repetition.
2   Dewey, *Experience and Education*, 52.
3   Ibid., 52.
4   Ibid., 53.
5   Dewey, *The Public and Its Problems*, 176.
6   Ibid.
7   Lisa Delpit, *Other People's Children*.
8   Dewey, *Experience and Education*, 54.
9   Kramer and Varenikova, "As Russia Retreats."
10 The are unstated ideas about gender implicit in all of this outrage and justification. Schools can be deemed less essential than firefighting only when someone else is available to take care of children instead, and that typically means mothers or other female kin. Additionally, women's cooperation with occupiers has historically been scrutinized with extreme suspicion when it touches on reproduction—sexual, but also cultural. In reactions to Ukrainian teachers who agreed to reopen elementary school classrooms, there are echoes of the extreme hostility directed toward young women who flirted or slept with German soldiers.
11 Kramer and Varenikova, "As Russia Retreats."
12 https://www.fsp.org/mission/ accessed 10/1/2022.
13 Hanson, "Croydon School Budget Set for Revote."
14 Barry, "One Small Step for Democracy."

REFERENCES

Allen, Danielle, *Talking to Strangers*. Chicago: University of Chicago Press, 2003.

Allen, Danielle, *Our Declaration*. New York: Norton, 2014.

Arendt, Hannah, "Collective Responsibility." In *Responsibility and Judgment*, ed. Jerome Kohn. New York: Schocken, 2003, pp. 147–58.

Arendt, Hannah, "Personal Responsibility under Dictatorship." In *Responsibility and Judgment*, ed. Jerome Kohn. New York: Schocken Books, 2003, pp. 194–211.

Aristotle, *Nicomachean Ethics*. Cambridge: Cambridge University Press, 2000.

Barnette, Kara, "Communities, Traitors, and the Feminist Cause: Looking toward Josaiah Royce for Feminist Scholarship." The Pluralist, v2 n2 Summer 2007, pp. 81–90.

Barry, Dan, "One Small Step for Democracy in a 'Live Free or Die' Town." *New York Times* (New York) July 10, 2022.

Cooper, John, "Aristotle on the Forms of Friendship." In *Reason and Emotion*. Princeton, NJ: Princeton University Press, 1999.

Deak, Kristof, *Mindenki* (Sing). http://www.singshortfilm.com.

Desan, Philippe, *Montaigne: A Life*. Princeton, NJ: Princeton University Press, 2017.

Dewey, John, *Democracy and Education*. New York: Free Press, 1916/1966.

Dewey, John, *Human Nature and Conduct*. New York: Henry Holt, 1922.

Dewey, John, *The Public and Its Problems*. Athens, OH: Ohio University Press, 1927/2016.

Dewey, John, *The School and Society*. Chicago: University of Chicago Press, 1938/1990.

Dewey, John, *Experience and Education*. New York: Simon and Schuster, 1938/1997.

Dunne, Joseph and Shirley Pendlebury, "Practical Reason." In *Blackwell Guide to the Philosophy of Education*, ed. Nigel Blake,

Paul Smeyers, Richard Smith and Paul Standish. Malden, MA: Blackwell, 2003, pp. 194–211.

Forster, E.M., "What I Believe." In *Two Cheers for Democracy*. New York: Harcourt, Brace and World, 1951.

Gines, Kathryn T., *Hannah Arendt and the Negro Question*. Bloomington: Indiana University Press, 2014.

Gordon, Mordechai, ed., *Hannah Arendt and Education: Renewing Our Common World*. Boulder, CO: Westview Press, 2001.

Hanson, Alex, "Croydon School Budget Set for Revote after It Was Slashed in Town Meeting." In *Concord Monitor* (Concord, NH), May 5, 2022. Accessed January 10, 2022.

Higgins, Chris, ed., "Education, Crisis, and the Human Condition: Arendt after 50 Years." *Teachers College Record* 112, no. 2 (2010).

Jaspers, Karl, *The Question of German Guilt*. New York: Fordham University Press, 1946/2001.

Kramer, Andrew E. and Maria Varenikova, "As Russia Retreats, a Question Lingers: Who Counts as a Collaborator?" *New York Times* (New York), September 22, 2022. Accessed September 22, 2022.

La Boétie, Étienne, *Discourse on Voluntary Servitude*, trans. James B. Atkinson and David Sices. Indianapolis: Hackett, 2012.

La Boétie, Étienne, *Discours de la Servitude Voluntaire*. https://fr.wikisource.org/wiki/Discours_de_la_servitude_volontaire/%C3%89dition_1922/Texte_entier.

Levinson, Meira, "Moral Injury and the Ethics of Educational Injustice." *Harvard Educational Review* 85, no. 2 (June, 2015), 203–28.

Levinson, Natasha, "But Some People Will Not: Arendtian Interventions in Education" *Philosophy of Education* (2002), pp. 200–8.

MacIntyre, Alisdair, *After Virtue*. South Bend, IN: University of Notre Dame Press, 1981.

Montaigne, Michel, *The Complete Works*, trans. Donald Frame. New York: Everyman's Library, 2003.

Nussbaum, Martha, *The Fragility of Goodness*. Cambridge: Cambridge University Press, 1986.

Pateman, Carol, *The Sexual Contract*. Redwood City, CA: Stanford University Press, 1988.

Plato, *Crito*, In *Plato: Five Dialogues* (Second edition), ed. John Cooper. Indianapolis: Hackett, 2001.

Rawls, John, *A Theory of Justice*. Cambridge, MA: Harvard University Press, 1971.

Rigolot, Francois, "Friendship and Voluntary Servitude: Plato, Ficino and Montaigne." *Texas Studies in Literature and Language*, Winter 2005 v47.

Rini, Regina, *The Ethics of Microaggression*. New York: Routledge, 2020.

Rowling, J.K., *Harry Potter and the Sorcerer's Stone*. New York: Scholastic, 1999.

Rowling, J.K., "The Fringe Benefits of Failure and the Importance of Imagination." https://news.harvard.edu/gazette/story/2008/06/text-of-j-k-rowling-speech/ accessed November 1, 2022.

Royce, Josiah, *The Philosophy of Loyalty*. New York: Macmillan, 1911.

Royce, Josiah, *War and Insurance*. New York: Macmillan, 1914.

Royce, Josiah, *The Hope of the Great Community*. New York: Macmillan, 1916.

Santoro, Doris, *Demoralized*. Cambridge, MA: Harvard Education Press, 2018.

Schutz, Aaron, "Is Political Education an Oxymoron?" *Philosophy of Education* (2001), pp. 324–32.

Schutz, Aaron, and Marie Sandy, "Friendship and the Public Stage: Revisiting Hannah Arendt's Resistance to 'Political Education.'" *Educational Theory* 65, no. 1 (2015), 21–38.

Sennett, Richard, *The Culture of the New Capitalism*. New Haven, CT: Yale University Press, 2007.

Shklar, Judith, *On Political Obligation*, ed. Samantha Ashenden and Andreas Hess. New Haven, CT: Yale University Press, 2019.

Shuffelton, Amy, "Collaboration: The Politics of Working Together." *Educational Theory* 68, no. 2 (2018), 147–60.

Smith, Richard, "Paths of Judgment: The Revival of Practical Wisdom." *Educational Theory and Practice* 31, no. 3 (1999), 327–40.

Stengel, Barbara, *Responsibility*. London: Bloomsbury, 2023.

Thoreau, Henry David, "Civil Disobedience." In *Henry David Thoreau: Collected Essays and Poems*, ed. Elizabeth Hall Witherell. Library of America, 2001.

Weber, Max, *The Protestant Ethic and the Spirit of Capitalism*. London: Routledge, 2001.

Young, Iris Marion, *Responsibility for Justice*. New York: Oxford University Press, 2006.

INDEX

adults responsibilities 57–8
agency 63, 65–6
Allen, Danielle 84 nn.15–16
Arendt, Hannah 9–10, 18,
   50–2, 90 n.20
   on collective responsibility
      55–8
   on guilt *versus* responsibility
      54, 59
   on moral and political
      responsibility 52–3
Aristotle
   civic friendships 26, 75
   civil conflict 23
   on friendships 15–16, 25–6,
      31, 85 n.6

character-based friendships. *See*
   personal friendship
citizens responsibility 53–4
civic friendship 16, 26, 41, 75
civil disobedience 31, 62,
   91 n.24
collaboration 9, 76
   activities 78–80
   best practices and 47–8
   competition and 60–1
   cooperation and 9–10, 60–1
   games and 69–72, 79
   good collaborators 67–8
   group projects 43
   inclination to 13–14
   in *Mindenki* 10–11, 48–9

under power/authorities
   11–12
power's effects on 49
responsibilities 49, 52–3
in school learning 4, 12,
   18–19, 21, 41–2, 80
Second World War 50–1, 60
colleague/collegiality 73–5
collective responsibility 17, 51,
   56–7, 90 n.12
   adults 57
   citizens' responsibilities 52
   moral and political
      responsibility 52–3
   moral guilt 56
   political/criminal guilt 55–7
compliance 61
consent 74–5
continuous experiences 44–5
cooperation and competition
   9–10, 60–1
Cooper, John 85 n.6
criminal guilt 55–6
"The Crisis in Education"
   (Arendt) 57
*The Culture of the New
   Capitalism* (Sennett) 66

democracy 5, 41
   friendship and 35, 84 n.16
   liberal 3
   society and 5, 7–8
   work/activity 9

Democracy and Education
    (Dewey) 5, 7, 9
Dewey, John
    on democracy 8–10, 15
    on experience 44–6
    on games and rules 76–7
    on society 5, 7–8, 38
*Discourse on Voluntary
    Servitude* (La Boétie)
    27–9, 32

education
    political thinking in 63–4
    practices/practical reasoning
        48
    social classrooms 78–9
    and society 5–7
educative experiences 44–7
Eichmann in Jerusalem
    (Arendt) 50–2
equality 14–15, 30–1, 76
ethical individualism 37
Experience and Education
    (Dewey) 7

faith in personal
    relationships 39–41
Forster, E. M. 23, 35, 39–41, 76
fraternity 14, 30–1, 75–7
French Wars of Religion 29
friendship(s) 15–16, 76,
        84 n.16, 85 n.6
    civic 16, 26, 41
    democracy and 35
    freedom 30–1
    in *Of Friendship* 23–5
    in *Harry Potter* 22, 24, 33
    liberty and equality 30–2
    loyalty 22–3, 28, 35–42
    personal 15–16, 25, 28, 35

reciprocal beneficence 25
    in school learning 21–2
"Friendship and Voluntary
    Servitude: Plato, Ficino
    and Montaigne"
    (Rigolot) 86 n.13

The Game of Village 69–72,
    79–80
group projects 43
groupwork 43, 50, 67
guilt 54–5
    moral 56
    political/criminal 55–7
    versus responsibility 54, 59

Harry Potter 16, 22, 24, 33
Hobbes, Thomas 30
The Human Condition (Arendt)
    9

ideal theory 6–7
interactive experiences 44–5

Jaspers, Karl 17, 51
    on guilt 54–7
    on power relations 61–2

Krakow 72–3, 75

La Boétie, Étienne de
    on freedom and equality
        30–2, 51, 76
    friendship of 23–30, 87 n.17
Learning to Labour (Willis)
    65
liberty 14–15, 30–1
    of self-expression 37
Locke, John 30
The Lord of the Flies 64

loyalty 6, 12
    causes to 36–8
    friendship and 28, 35–6
    love and 40

Madison, James 63
metaphysical guilt 56
Milgram, Stanley 51
Mindenki 1, 3, 8, 10–11, 48–9,
    80
miseducative experience 45–6,
    49
Montaigne, Michel de
    friendship of 23–5, 27–30
    on La Boétie's writing 29, 32
    moral and political
        responsibility 52–3
moral guilt 56

national unity 14
nativism 3
Nazis 11, 51–4, 78, 90 n.12
New Hampshire 72–3, 75,
    82–3
1984 (Orwell) 54

obedience 63
Of Friendship (Montaigne)
    23–5

personal friendship 15–16, 25,
    28, 35
personal responsibility 59
The Philosophy of Loyalty
    (Royce) 38, 88 n.34
Poland 72–3
political/criminal guilt 55–6
power relations 61–2, 71, 76
    agency and 63
    organizing 65

practices/practical reasoning
    46–8
The Public and Its Problems
    (Dewey) 8–9

The Question of German Guilt
    (Jaspers) 17, 54–5

racial discrimination 57
Rawls, John 6
"Reflections on Little Rock"
    (Arendt) 57
Republic (Plato) 7
responsibility(ies) 4, 12, 18–19
    citizens 53–4
    collective (*See* collective
        responsibility)
    guilt *versus* 54–7, 59
    moral and political 52–3
    mutual 49
    personal 59
Rigolot, Francois 86 n.13
Rousseau, Jean-Jacques 30
Rowling, J. K. 22, 85 n.1
Royce, Josiah
    on beautiful community 41
    on loyalty 23, 35–40,
        87 n.29, 88 nn.34–5
Russo-Ukrainian War 80–2

The School and Society
    (Dewey) 5, 9
school learning
    activities 79
    on collaboration 4, 12, 21
    friendship 21–2
    good collaborators 67–8
    school budget 82–3
self-development and loyalty
    37

Sennett, Richard 66
sentimentalism 77
Shklar, Judith 22, 85 n.2
social classrooms 78–9
The Social Contract and *Émile*
    (Rousseau) 7
social control 76
social group 7
society 5
    democracy and 5, 7–8
    education and 5–7
Socrates 62–3
solidarity 14, 23, 65, 76

technical reasoning 46–7
Thoreau, Henry David 63
totalitarianism 50, 52–4,
    81
town meeting 72–3, 82–3

Two Cheers for Democracy
    (Royce) 41

Ukraine's education 80–2
United States' *Declaration of
    Independence* 74

Village game program. *See* The
    Game of Village
Voluntary Servitude (La Boétie)
    74

Willis, Paul 65–6
workplaces 66–7
    collegiality in 74
World War II 11, 17, 40, 50–1,
    60

Young, Iris Marion 17, 58–60